THE HOLY LAND
CONTEMPORARY VISIONS
AND SCRIPTURES

THE HOLY LAND

CONTEMPORARY VISIONS
AND SCRIPTURES

EDITED BY

ITHAMAR HANDELMAN-SMITH

Published by Repeater Books
An imprint of Watkins Media Ltd

19-21 Cecil Court
London
WC2N 4EZ
UK
www.repeaterbooks.com
A Repeater Books Paperback Original 2017
1

Distributed in the United States by Random House, Inc.,
New York.

Cover design: Johnny Bull
Typography and typesetting: Josse Pickard
Typefaces: Hoefler Text

ISBN: 978-1-910924-58-7
EBOOK ISBN: 978-1-910924-60-0

CONTENTS

PART TWO: KEDMA

*(Translates both as "east" and as "progress" or "forward-facing",
as the ancient Israelites looked at the east instead of today's
north. Alshrq in Arabic.)*

PART THREE: TZAFONA

(In ancient Hebrew the north was called Tzafona or Semola, meaning "left", which is like the Arabic Shamal, as in "north".)

PART FOUR: NEGEB

(Negeb or Timna is the southern desert, meaning "south" in ancient Hebrew. Janub in Arabic.)

INTRODUCTION
by Ithamar Handelman-Smith

Israel is not a country; it is not even, as someone has suggested, a state of mind. It is simply a disorderly systematic collection of paradoxes that somehow seem to make sense - don't ask me to explain how. Whatever you may say about Israel or Israelis, the opposite is equally true: every man, woman or child seems to be mobilised for war, yet every time they want to say hello, goodbye, how's your grandmother, or what's up, they say shalom, which means peace; and in a crazy way they make you believe they mean it. Here is no aristocracy of rank or wealth, not even a sense of rank in their army, not because they are so democratic but because everyone here thinks he's a general. And the greatest paradox of them all is that I, Roy Hemmings, have got myself stuck here, to report on a war that will not take place...

With this monologue, director-turned-rabbi (read Dana Kessler's beautiful essay "*Metzizim*") Uri Zohar, one of Israel's best known artists of all time, decided to open his 1968 film, *Every Bastard a King*.

The film is an exceptional and unique description of the Israeli-Arabic conflict; told from the point of view of Roy Hemmings, a Hemingway-esque American journalist reporting from Israel and the Palestinian (then Jordanian) territories. It is the eve of the Six-Day War, a pivotal point in the modern history of this land. Through these foreign eyes, Zohar examines the complexity of this story, the story of Israel and Palestine, even before the actual occupation. The story of the Holy Land.

Throughout history, this little piece of land in the southern Levant, stretching between the sea and the Jordan River, has had many different names: there was the biblical pagan land of Canaan, then it was the Promised Land (or simply Eretz Israel) that God promised Abraham, and there were the ancient Jewish kingdoms of Israel (Samaria) and Judah. In the Babylonian and Persian period, the land was referred to as the province of Yehud Medinata, and under Hellenistic occupation it was Coele-Syria. The Romans called it the Province of Judea, and under the Byzantine Empire it was known as Palaestina Prima. The many different Arab and Muslim conquerors gave it many different names (Al-Urdunn, Filastin etc.) and the crusaders named it the Latin Kingdom of Jerusalem. Under the Ottoman Empire it was known mainly as part of Greater Syria. Then it was the British Mandatory Palestine, and eventually the state of Israel. But all along, it was the Holy Land: for Jews, Christians and Muslims alike.

As Zohar wrote, it "is not a country, it is not even, as someone has suggested, a state of mind", but a "collection of paradoxes" that "somehow seem to make sense". In this anthology of short fiction, poetry, essays and artworks, we try to make a bit more sense out of it all. While offering no specific political solution to the ongoing conflict over this, we try to put together diverse reflections and personal and subjective perspectives in order to shed some more light on the different places and landscapes of the Holy Land. We try to give voice to the many different communities living here, in this land today, from secular to orthodox Jewish Israelis through to Muslim and Christian Palestinians, the

Circassians of the north and the Bedouin of the south. This is a kaleidoscope through which the reader might be able to see the Holy Land in new light and colour.

PART ONE: YAMA

(In ancient Hebrew: "the sea", meaning "west".
Gharb in Arabic)

HOUSE OF THE WISE AT HEART
by Shlomzion Kenan

The heart of the wise is in the house of mourning;
But the heart of fools is in the house of mirth.
(Ecclesiastes 7:4)

One afternoon in the autumn of 1832, a young Arab horseman was hunting for gazelle in the swamplands that stretched beyond the citrus groves of Jaffa when he chanced upon a traveller. Recognising him immediately, the young horseman rode up to greet him, introducing himself (as Alphonse de Lamartine will later recount in his *Voyage en Orient*), in Italian, as an Arab; Italian by origin; French at heart. His father, he said, the French Consul to Jaffa, a certain Monsieur Damiani, has heard about the imminent arrival of the famous Frenchman and would like to warmly welcome him as a guest at his home.

Around that time, the reign of the "modern father of Jaffa"–the Turkish Sultan's governor, Muhammad Abu-Nabbut–was drawing to a close. During his fifteen years as governor, Abu-Nabbut rebuilt Jaffa for the hundredth time, after a hundred devastations, this time around as an imposing, prosperous, commercial, multicultural port town. A year prior to Lamartine's visit, as the Egyptian Mohammad Ali moved in, he fled to Mecca. Ten years earlier, a North African Jewish community began to prosper in the Old City.

One traveller concluded in 1823 that the fruit of the city were each larger than a man's fist and that no man could carry its red, sweet watermelons. So Lamartine was invited to Damiani's beautiful home, where the breeze, thick and salty, entered through the paneless windows, rattling the chandeliers. Lamartine has a street named after him in Jaffa to this day. Damiani, the hospitable consul, doesn't.

Two years ago, crowded out of Tel Aviv by booming real estate prices, I moved to Jaffa, to the top two floors of what was once a one-family home and is now a quietly dilapidating six-family home. It was still grand, though. With the five-point star, symbol of the Ottoman Empire, sculpted in crumbling clay above the front door. Tile roofed, perched on a hill, its cedar wood shutters and portholes were fixed upon the Mediterranean that was surely and quickly being eclipsed by construction and gentrification. The two chickens I saw in the alleyway on the first day belonged to a fisherman whose Bedouin family had fished in the waters of Jaffa for seven generations. From their rickety fishing boat they saw the battleships of Napoleon sailing in. After the Nakba (the Palestinian term for the exodus during the 1948 war)–with the original landlords turned refugees–the father moved into this house and added a few rooms to it, down where the stables must have once been. The other five residents of the house did more or less the same throughout the 1950s. Like ground squirrels that move into dens meerkats have vacated, one by one they moved in–some by orders from the state, others by orders of the gut or heart. They erected new walls between them, dividing the place up, de-gentrifying it, keeping what they lost private and letting the gossip pour out into the alleyway publicly. Three Muslims, one Christian-

Armenian and two Jews. Up until some of them sold and moved on or died, all were refugees or sons and daughters of refugees whose story had been written and archived by a state of refugees that had made refugees of others.

There were some bright tracksuits drying, bellowing in the wind, up the front, on that first day I moved in, and through a creaky, battered double blue door, I entered the high limestone-walled courtyard, with its stooped, dusty birds of paradise, its dried out pond, and the lemon tree that arched over from the churchyard across the wall. The windows were dreamily draped with ancient bougainvillea in pink, white and purple, but the trademark Jaffa floor tiles had been pulled out decades earlier by previous tenants who wanted to ease themselves into the erasure of the past.

When I went to City Hall to fetch the blueprints of the house, I found a crumpled 1947 scroll with a beautiful sketch of the house and the name of its owner scribbled in handwritten Arabic on top: Hanna Damiani—prosperous landowner and proprietor of the olive oil soap factory at the old Turkish Serail building.

It was this Hanna Damiani's great-grandfather who welcomed Alphonse de Lamartine in 1832, dressed in a sky-blue double-buttoned kaftan and a crimson silk belt which Lamartine found to be "grotesque" and "oriental". Could they have been chatting away in French and Italian amidst silver trays and Chinese porcelain right here, where I am now sitting and writing this, looking out towards Andromeda's Rock? Probably not. My home, at the Maronite section of Ajami, south of the Old City gates, was most likely built no sooner than the late nineteenth century.

It stands to reason, then, that it could not have been the same home in which an older ancestor of Monsieur Damiani hosted Napoleon Bonaparte in the spring of 1799, just between the latter killing a few thousand people who bled into the sea, asking his doctor to poison with opium those who had to be left behind, and failing to conquer Acre and become emperor of the east.

But the young lad who rode his horse in the swamps that day and ushered the travel-weary Frenchman through the groves, towards the 130-foot lush green hill from which the Old City of Jaffa once cascaded into the sea, was certainly one of Hanna Damiani's ancestors, an illustrious family of diplomats and consuls for France, England and Italy, whose coat of arms once adorned the ceiling of my next-door neighbour's carved wooden ceiling until it was painted over.

Like all things beautiful and exquisite, Jaffa has been ravaged, ransacked, taken, loved, destroyed and rebuilt dozens of times over four millennia. Pirates and pilgrims dubbed it a Belvedere of Joy. Palestinian refugees cherish it as their Bride of the Sea. As old as the Bronze Age, Jaffa is one of the oldest and most important ports on the Via Mare. Its name, some say, is a tribute to Noah's son Yeffet. Others say it predates the flood. In Hellenistic tradition, it was Joppa or Iopeia, after Andromeda's mother, Cassiopeia. In the language of the Sidonians it was Yaffa, the beautiful. According to Lamartine there were roughly five thousand people living in Jaffa in the 1830s: Turks, Armenians, Greeks, Maronites and Catholics. Of a population of seventy thousand Palestinians living in Jaffa in 1948 (not counting surrounding villages), it is assumed that three thousand remain. For the most part, they were gathered up from the Old City and the Casba and locked up in Ajami, where martial law was instated until the 1960s.

A race of particularly short people once hunted for rhinos in its oak woods, centuries before the sky was lost to housing developments flanked by drug stops and asbestos huts, embittered by wars of class, nation and religion. The multicultural Terra Irredenta, Palestine's lost Shambala, the colonial idea of paradise, had turned into purgatory. Still very much the Provence of the Middle East to the large international community living here, but scratch the surface and there's that beautiful, harsh, crazy, old, trendy, peaceful, warful, chaotic, regal, rundown, conflicted hill on the water some call home. Indeed, the Jaffa of 2013 I moved into is a far and bitter cry from the city the romantic one Lamartine visited in 1832. He describes coming upon a hill that looms over the turquoise waves, covered in oak, citrus, fir, and pomegranate trees, streaked with freshwater streams that flowed through a row of jutting capes into the sea. Rows of firs protected the fruit trees from the harsh sea winds and church bells carried on the magic air. Jaffa, he wrote, offers "the perfect haven of repose for the life-weary man who wants nothing but to enjoy a benevolent sun".

In the spring of 1948, Hanna Damiani left his Jaffa home–perhaps my home–perhaps by boat, perhaps by land, never to return. Did he leave the stove on? Did he take a key? Did he keep it all these years? I know that some Irgun soldiers, some who were recently liberated from the camps, were seen looting enormous crystal chandeliers from the palatial villas of the Maronite neighbourhood, holding them in their arms and running. Small, frightened men with the bright blue sea and the yellow sun reflected a million times in their arms.

The Assyrians conquered Jaffa from the Philistines, who conquered it from the Egyptians. In the eleventh century, the Muslims destroyed it to prevent the crusaders from seizing it. Two centuries later, it was destroyed again by the Mamluks.

Canaanites, Ethiopians, Philistines, Egyptians, Assyrians,

Greeks, Jews, Romans, Muslims, Mamluks, English, French, Turks, Israelis. Flavius Josephus had seen Andromeda's shackles still attached to the rock. He had seen the wind of the black north tear ships in half, serendipitously for the Romans, who were able to take Jaffa over from the Jews without a struggle and "turn it into a wasteland".

During the second century BC Jaffa was annexed to the Hasmonean kingdom, a synagogue was built in the eighteenth century, and long before that, a thousand devastations ago, King Solomon brought cedar trees from Lebanon to Jaffa to build his temple in Jerusalem. The Jewish traveller, Rabbi Itzhak Chelo, wrote in 1334 that Jaffa's main trades are olive oil, cotton wool, scented soaps, glass bowls, dried fruit. The Jews of this town, he wrote, have a splendid synagogue with precious old books, but few can read.

In the late nineteenth century, when my house, along with other Christian-Maronite homes to the south of the Old City were built, Jaffa was an international, bustling, cultured, commercial port town, with oranges, ships, cinemas, theatres, hospitals, schools and hotels. Today, there are no ships, no oranges, no hotels, no cinemas, no theatres—just secure housing, slums, drug-stops, the trendy bars of the flea market and orientalist tourist attractions. Yaffa, the beautiful, is losing its good looks. It's hard to tell how the Pizzeans or the Franks, the Turks or the Egyptians, rebuilt Jaffa after its numerous devastations, but I'm pretty sure that the Israelis, after having levelled the Casbah and other parts of Jaffa in 1948, did one of the worse jobs. While the Old City and some Ottoman-era buildings are being beautifully restored and preserved, some new tenement buildings erected along the Ajami coast look like they could use a hint from history's penchant for demolition. If Abu-Nabbut, the Turk, rebuilt modern Jaffa and made it flourish, Ron Huldai, the residing mayor of Tel Aviv-Yafo, is responsible for gentrifying it. Indeed, Jaffa appears to be the only case of gentrification in the world that has kept the criminal classes–bred and nurtured by decades of calculated neglect–intact and abloom. This, after Huldai's predecessor, Shlomo Lahat, had turned Jaffa into a permanent demolition site. During the Seventies and Eighties, the palatial mansions of Ajami were systematically demolished to prevent absentees from returning. The debris was then piled high along the beach to deny the denizens their view of the sea. Finally, with the idea–either, as some say, inspired by a planned conspiracy, or by natural market forces–to bring more Jews to Jaffa and boost up the prices, the debris was covered up in earth and grass and turned into a park. Nowadays, the sea view is slowly hidden–not by garbage, but by the rich. And the skies of Jaffa, once lacerated by steeples and minarets, are also lost. Darkened.

It was the Armenian lady, who lives downstairs with her dog, who first told me about the gold. According to her, it was her late husband, or maybe a relation of her late husband, who, shortly after the Nakba, met a refugee from Jaffa in Lebanon. This refugee, perhaps a member of the Damiani family, perhaps not, described the house and explained precisely where the wall was in which he had buried the gold. It is the porous limestone wall that now surrounds my limestone patio, with an old lemon tree stooping forth, as sweet and as sour as the longings for what Jaffa was. I don't know if the Armenian family came to Jaffa in pursuit of the gold, or perhaps they came to work with Abu George, the French company's lighthouse attendant up until 1966–or was he already living in Jaffa? At any rate, one night he started hitting the wall with a sledgehammer. He looked for a weak spot and sure enough, after a while he heard a metallic sound and hit a hard place. The jackpot came pouring out, glittering in the moonlight. Hearing all the racket, the upstairs neighbours, the Jewish immigrants from Iraq who sold the place after fifty years to a real estate investor who sold it to me, came down and, seeing what was what, called the police. The Armenian was arrested for three days and then released, with the gold, which he had to split up with the other families living in the house.

Nothing else was split very evenly. Except, perhaps, exile and dislocation. The mother of the Jewish-Iraqi family, who lived for fifty-odd years in the same apartment in which I'm living now, always wore slippers outside. This, the neighbours thought, was a constant reminder of the last time she left her home in Iraq, and like Damiani, had locked the door for the last time, then, after having seen her father dragged through the streets, walked by foot to Israel. Next door to her (and as of recently, to me) lives a German Jew with her all too familiar German Jewish story, and downstairs, for another fifty-odd years, still lives another Palestinian-Arab family, whose village was demolished in 1948. Though they have some family members in jail, some assassinated and some in rehab, the women of the house are always laughing, always watering the herbs outside, trying to make things grow. Once, there was a Muslim cat lady living on her own downstairs. The cats were buried in my patio, next to the wall where the gold was found, and the woman was buried in a cemetery, and the house was auctioned and bought by one of Jaffa mobsters who, like many others, had discovered the newly lucrative avenue of real estate-related crime. One day, he too broke down the wall with a sledgehammer. Not for gold, but for installing a door in the patio and thus bettering his investment. Like the calcareous sandstone Jaffa is made of, these stories, past and present, are filled with holes. Their matter is porous. Weathered. Patinated by time, sedimented by water, legends sieved through them, tall tales, tragedies, like a nebulous fishnet they ebb and flake off through the centuries. Andromeda, Jonah, St Peter: one is now a gentrified, doorman-secure real-estate-swimming-pool-project, one a high-end port restaurant, the third still a church.

British journalist Robert Fisk tracked down David Damiani, Hanna Damiani's son, in Beirut, and interviewed him for a book. David told him about his ancestor Boutros Damiani, who was born in Jerusalem in 1687. His four sons were consuls in Jaffa for Britain, France, Holland and Tuscany. The last consul in the Damiani family was Ferdinand, he writes, who represented Mexico in 1932. In the days of Napoleon, it was Anton Damiani who interceded on behalf of the Muslim community. According to Fisk's interview, David Damiani had only just moved into a new home with his new wife shortly before 1948. One day, on the third week of April, they left their home for the last time and locked the front door behind them just before lunchtime. They carried only one suitcase, a jewellery case and the registry deeds to their lands and got on a boat to Beirut.

After conducting this interview, Fisk travelled to Jaffa and found the house that was once David Damiani's. Living there now was Israeli sculptor Shlomo Green, a Holocaust survivor who had lost a hundred relatives in Auschwitz. After learning about the Damianis and their story, of how David Damiani stood at the stern on the ship leaving the Jaffa port wishing he could turn around, the sculptor "looked up quite suddenly with tears in his eyes and said, 'I am very moved by what you have told me... what can I say? I would like to meet these people, if you can say for me...'" Here,

Fisk writes, he paused, and then said:

> 'It's a tragedy of both our people. How can I explain in my poor
> English? I think the Arabs have the same rights as the Jews and
> I think it is a tragedy of history that a people who are refugees
> make new refugees. I have nothing against the Arabs... They are
> the same as us. I don't know that we Jews did this tragedy–but
> it happened.'

In Beirut, Fisk told Damiani about what Green had said,
writing, "I repeated the details of how so many of Green's
family had been murdered at Auschwitz. Damiani showed
no bitterness. 'I wish him happiness,' he said."

I don't think, however, that the current descendants of
the illustrious family feel the same way. I have tried to make
contact with them, first through Fisk, whom I was told
does not respond to Israelis, then through a go-betweener
from Jaffa, who had sent my letter through London to
Beirut, where he was assured that it had reached the three
grandchildren of Hanna Damiani. An answer did not come.

Ramses II, Cleopatra, Pompeius, Alexander the Great,
Saladin Richard the Lionheart, Napoleon, Abu-Nabbut,
Mohammad Ali, Selim the Grim, and now us israeli, loved
it, ruined it and rebuilt it, and some day it will be ruined
again. When the crusaders went on a new conquest spree
in the 1300s, the Ottoman Sultan decided to take no further
risk and demolished Jaffa to the ground. He left no stone on
stone and blocked down the port. John Polloner, a traveller
in 1422, discovered a ruined city, empty of men, without one
house standing, except the ruins of St Peter's church. De La
Brockierre, a French traveller, wrote in 1432: "I have never
seen such destruction anywhere else, and I am puzzled at
how they were able to topple such thick walls."

These walls, the thick walls of this house, can crumble even if they are strong. They are made of empty cavities and stories. They can crash to reveal a grave, a treasure, a door. Their stories can become histories in the same way that men and women become communities and nations. But it is up to the people–not the nations and what they have done–to choose which way the souls of this purgatory wish to go. To mend the walls of their homes and tear down the ones in their hearts. Even as the same stories keep repeating themselves throughout the eons, with one in particular that stands out above the rest.

The one about the virgin bride of the sea and her wedding night. Since before the flood she had been beautiful. But time and again, when her orchard beds are strewn white with citrus blossoms, her streets wash red with blood.

BIBLIOGRAPHY

Aldor, Gaby (Hebrew), *The Lane of White Chairs*, play produced by the Arab-Hebrew Theatre of Jaffa (1989)

Fisk, Robert, *Pity the Nation: The Abduction of Lebanon*, Nation Books, New York (1990)

De Lamartine, Alphonse, *Voyage en Orient*, Paris (1835)

Lebore, Adam, *City of Oranges: An Intimate History of Arabs and Jews in Jaffa*, ww Norton & Company, London/New York (2007)

Shezaf, Tzur (Hebrew), *A Guide to Jaffa*, shezaf.net

Tolkowsky, Samuel (Hebrew), *A History of Jaffa*, Dvir, Jerusalem (1926)

Original poster for *Metzizim*, 1972

METZIZIM
by Dana Kessler

Nobody remembers exactly when, but at some point the popular beach located at the northern edge of Tel Aviv's sea shore changed its name from Sheraton Beach to Metzitzim Beach. It probably happened around the time that *Metzitzim*–a once forgotten cinematic gem from the early Seventies–suddenly started to develop a huge cult following, as well as recognition as one of Israel's best-loved movies of all time.

More than forty years after its initial release, *Metzitzim* (or *Peeping Toms* as it is known outside of Israel) is considered by many as the greatest film in the history of Israeli cinema. This is one of the few cases in which film critics and mass audiences agree on a movie, but it is probably just because when they watch *Metzitzim* they see two very different films.

Metzitzim revolves around a gang of adult men who refuse to grow up. Imagine the Mediterranean version of Richard Linklater's or Kevin Smith's slackers, or maybe Seinfeld's gang years before Gen X reared its ugly head. Gutte (played by Uri Zohar, who also directed the film) and Eli (Arik Einstein, who wrote the script with Zohar) are two thirtysomething beach bums. Being best friends, they do all they can to help each other stay submerged in a constant state of denial about the fact that they really should begin to take responsibility for their lives.

They hang out at the beach, looking to get laid and pulling silly pranks. Eli, a good-looking musician, has a loving and very cute wife and a little girl at home, but prefers to hang out with Gutte at the beach, constantly whining about his life and blatantly disregarding the vows he took, probably not very long ago. As Einstein once described him: "He's a little dreck".

Gutte works as a lifeguard and lives in a shack on the beach, which he lets Eli use for his sexual escapades. Although a big part of his everyday chores is to drive away the voyeurs who come to the beach to catch a glimpse of what goes on inside the ladies' showers, Gutte can't resist a peek through the wall whenever Eli picks up a groupie after playing a club gig.

Today *Metzitzim* is a part of Israeli history, and a landmark of Tel Aviv culture. It was the first of three Zohar films that are known as the Tel Aviv trilogy, along with *Einayim Gdolot* (*Big Eyes*), which also paired Zohar with Einstein in the leading roles and might even be superior to *Metzitzim* in quality (but certainly not in popularity), and *Hatzilu Et HaMatzil* (*Save the Lifeguard*), Zohar's last film, which seems like a dumbed-down version of *Metzitzim*, done in terribly poor taste.

These days you'd be hard pressed to find an Israeli who hasn't seen *Metzitzim* at least once or twice or a hundred times. While the old shack from the movie has been demolished by the local government and the beach has been renovated to cater to families rather than the wayward teenagers who used to frequent it, bored soldiers still amuse themselves by quoting naughty lines from the film (one thing you should know about Israeli soldiers is their undying love of Israeli cult films), while aging bohemians with cracked tans boast about being extras in it in their long-lost youth.

It is hard to believe today, but when *Metzitzim* was first released, the masses didn't flock to see it. Many excuses have been made over the years for this failure—excuses that blossomed into myth. Since Israeli mythology usually has something to do with one war or another, some people believe *Metzitzim* failed because it was released immediately before the Yom Kippur War. But since ten months had passed from the film's premiere at the now defunct Orly Movie Theatre in Tel Aviv (on which—true to cliché—a parking lot now stands) until the Arab coalition launched its surprise attack, that excuse doesn't really hold water.

Another explanation—perhaps more plausible than the first—is that *Metzitzim* is a summer movie (even though it doesn't have the mandatory summer movie happy ending) released in winter. While no one in their right mind would release *Grease* in December, dragging the audience out in the cold to see Zohar sweat his hairy ass off at the beach probably wasn't the best of ideas. Apart from that, most of Israel's movie-goers probably weren't ready at the time for Zohar's dirty mouth and filthy behaviour. When accused of blatant and unnecessary vulgarity in an interview a few weeks after *Metzitzim*'s release, Zohar quoted one of his idols, Lenny Bruce, who said, "If God created the Body, and the Body is dirty, then the fault lies with the Manufacturer."

Apart from being well received at the 23rd Berlin International Film Festival, where it entered the competition in June 1973, *Metzitzim* was pretty much forgotten for many years. It resurfaced in the Eighties at midnight screenings in art-house cinemas in Tel Aviv, and together with the help of the VCR, it started to gain the cult status it enjoys today.

Metzitzim initially bombed even though Zohar and Einstein were key figures in Israel's entertainment industry. Both were all-round entertainers, who did pretty much everything in the biz. Zohar was a popular actor, comedian (sometimes credited as being Israel's first stand-up comic) and entertainer. And while his TV career was often of the embarrassingly mainstream kind (at one point he hosted Israel's first game show–a local version of *I've Got a Secret*), he always strived to be a serious film director, and indeed an auteur.

Before making *Metzitzim*, Zohar already had an impressive filmography under his belt, ranging from satirical comedies to very personal modernistic films influenced by the French New Wave. At first Zohar, like many international directors, adopted the method of "one for the money, one for the soul" (while most of the time the one for the money was made to recuperate the losses from the one for the soul). But it seems that with *Metzitzim* he actually tried to combine the two, merging two opposing genres that traditionally appealed to two very different types of audiences.

Einstein–a singer, actor and comedian–was no less of a star, and is to this day considered Israel's greatest male singer of all time. In the early Seventies Zohar and Einstein collaborated on the sketch-and-song TV show *Lool* (*The Chicken Coop*), which also eventually became a cult hit. The show's creators and cast became known as the Lool Gang, and together they produced Einstein's albums at the time and a couple of movies, one of them being *Metzitzim*.

The Lool Gang is remembered not only for its art, but also for its lifestyle. Zohar, Einstein, Shalom Hanoch (Israel's prime rocker, who wrote the music for *Metzitzim*) and their friends will forever be credited–or blamed–for bringing the Sixties to the Jewish state. They brought the sound, the look (it's hard to say they were hippies exactly, but they did sport an unkempt style and long hair), the drugs, and above all–the spirit of free love. Together with a handful of albums, movies and other cultural artefacts, *Metzitzim* became a symbol of late-Sixties and early-Seventies Tel Aviv bohemia. Of course, it didn't hurt that the film's starlet and sex symbol, Mona Zilberstein–who made her mark on celluloid with the sexy scene in which Zohar hoses her sandy body off–later died of a heroin overdose.

For today's audience, *Metzitzim* is pure nostalgia. A large part of the film's charm lies in its local colour, in the way it authentically captures a certain moment in the history of Tel Aviv. The film's believable characters, the use of non-actors in the cast and Adam Greenberg's superb cinematography (before he emigrated to the US and was later nominated for an Academy Award for his work on *Terminator 2: Judgment Day*) make up a large part of *Metzitzim*'s realistic charm. As *Haaretz*'s film critic at the time, Yosef Shrick, beautifully put it when it was first released: "Adam Greenberg's camera followed the gang around as if it were a stray dog." Anything Gutte, Eli and their friends did or said–no matter how vulgar or shocking–the camera loved. And that's the magic of cinema: what the camera loves, the viewer can't help but fall in love with too.

Metzitzim was atmospheric and, of course, funny. At first glance it is a hilarious comedy, with enough vulgarity to match *American Pie*, but *Metzitzim* is much more than a cult phenomenon or a piece of Israeli nostalgia. As Einstein has pointed out many times, the film was, and still is, very much misunderstood. Since it combined elements of the two opposing genres that dominated Israeli cinema at the time–the popular comic melodramas known as Bourekas films and the personal films that critics loved but the public ignored–it is no surprise that the audience didn't exactly know what to make of it. But watching it today, it is impossible to escape its persistent, and almost depressing, melancholic undercurrent. Under the film's light façade lies Gutte's heartbreaking loneliness, and the feeling that even if the Sixties were a glorious time of freedom and frivolity, the emptiness of this hedonistic lifestyle left quite a few souls deeply wounded.

Looking back at Zohar's well-documented biography and the history of Israeli society, it is clear that what might seem a light-hearted comedy about a gang of useless beach bums is in fact a harsh manifestation of the inevitable identity crisis the Jewish nation faced a quarter of a century after its foundation. At the heart of *Metzitzim* lies the deep existential crisis that Zohar went through in his personal life, one that characterised his entire generation. Not only were the new Israelis—born in the late Thirties and Forties—devoid of the Zionist passion of their immigrant parents who came to Palestine to build their people a homeland, they also neglected to fulfil their parents' expectations. Instead of the strong collective that Israel was founded upon, *Metzitzim* shows a group of lost individuals with empty lives who swapped the lofty ideals of their parents for cheap thrills—some booze and a roll in the sand with a banana model, or at least a peek at it through a hole in the wall.

While in America the Sixties ethos of free love was accompanied by anti-war protests, in Israel it reeked of escapism. *Metzitzim* came out just before the end of the Six-Day War euphoria, and just before the trauma of the Yom Kippur War. In those days (almost) no one in their right mind would protest against Israel's military actions. Zohar and his friends weren't into fighting, and they weren't into the Ashkenazi bourgeois life that was expected of them either. They preferred to hang out at the beach as if they were carefree teenagers. The only problem was that they were much too old for that. Einstein once told an interviewer that a film critic who had written about *Metzitzim* when it was first released claimed it was ridiculous that he and Zohar played the roles of beach boys at their age, but–as Einstein pointed out–that was the whole point. It was high time for them–and for Israel–to grow up.

Gutte and Eli's disregard for the establishment and bourgeoisie can easily be compared to the disillusionment with the American Dream seen in movies like *Easy Rider* and *Midnight Cowboy* just a few years before. But of course, this is the Israeli version, and in real life Zohar found a very Jewish solution to his problem.

Many believe that the aimless existence of *Metzitzim*'s protagonists–based on some level or other on the Lool Gang's real life–eventually made Zohar a *hozer betshuva* (literally "one who came back with an answer", meaning turned to Orthodox Judaism). At the peak of his success, Zohar decided to trade in the spotlight for a brighter light, as did quite a few of his friends and peers from Tel Aviv's bohemian scene (Einstein's ex-wife and children also became Orthodox Jews at the same time, and Einstein's two daughters eventually married Zohar's two sons). Abandoning their parents' ideals must have created quite a father complex for Zohar's generation, thus turning to God was only to be expected.

In 1977, Zohar retired from show business and moved to a Yeshiva (a university-like religious school) in Jerusalem and became a rabbi. The only reminders of his former life were the commercials which he directed for Shas–an ultra-orthodox religious political party–as part of its election campaign.

As *Metzitzim* clearly shows–at least to whomever cares to see more than the film's horny exterior–Zohar was part of a lost generation, one that struggled to find new meaning for life, having lost the one its parents had. Zohar was impatient and turned to God. Had he waited a couple of decades, the mind-numbing capitalistic rat race that finally caught up with Israel might have given him–as it did the rest of Israel's secular population–a new *raison d'être*.

FRIDAY AFTERNOON AT THE MERSAND CAFÉ
by Rana Werbin

So Ynet says that Orthodox women are finally fed up with getting married in their late teens and then giving birth every year till their forties.

Like that'll help them much. The chances of them being able to avoid pregnancy subjugation are equal to the chance that all women sitting around us here today will have the nerve to go around braless. We talk about it, bitch about it, send each other Facebook cards saying "Home is where the bra comes off," but we all know we won't dare to actually do it. There was a time in the Seventies… but then everyone was young and perky-breasted. It wouldn't have worked with the older women. No one can be that liberal. Anyway, that time is gone now. It's all rounded cups now, wherever you go.

I still sometimes go braless, Sarah! Or with an unwired, uncapped bra. And I'm no spring chicken, I'm about to turn forty soon! My God.

But you only go without a bra when you wear something so tight that it holds 'em up nicely. Admit it!

I do. But that's just because I'm not even.

I'm not even either, so what! And mine are larger and droopier than yours. It took me over a year before I went braless around Avi. And that's even though he sees me in bed naked almost every night. Still, I just couldn't face him bare-breasted under a loose shirt. I was afraid he'd be disgusted. A year! Let's face it, we wear our bras like our great-grandmothers wore their bodices, like the modern intellectual Arab women wear a hijab, like the national-religious young married women wear a smartly tied scarf showing just a tiny allowed bit of hair in the front. We all conform, and we fool ourselves to think that just having this little something around your head or around your tits is way better than covering yourself up entirely in a burka or shaving your head to wear a wig or squeezing your intestines in a whale-boned corset, and that we've advanced so much. We're lying to ourselves, Rana, not just to the men we fear won't find us attractive anymore if we disobey the rules.

But anyway, we're always lying to ourselves, don't you think, Sarah? I mean, even if we all walked around with our tits shaking about freely, our wombs vacant and carefree, hair wild and loose, and even if men were still somehow attracted to us, maybe because all the perky twenty-year-olds were already taken, and we would never ever be shamed for looking as we naturally do—even then, we would still lie to ourselves and shut our eyes to oppression. Only we'd be lying about other things, that's all. All people lie to themselves, all the time.

Are you gonna talk about politics again? I thought we agreed it's an off subject on weekends!

No! Fine! Even though it's all politics, you know. But, no, ok, don't give me that look, I promise, no Eritrean refugees, Chinese labourers or Palesti—

Hey, speaking of, what happened with Saleh, did he ever answer your text?

No.

No?

No. I don't really want to talk about it.

Fine, we don't have to. But I thought for sure he was going to text you back after—

Hey! I said I don't wanna talk about it. Can we please change the subject!? Let's just talk about work, OK?

FRIDAY EVENING AT MINZAR

God, Rana, I'm just so sick of being poor and having to work for money. I just wish I could do what I like and make a decent living out of it. I don't even need much. I simply want to not hate my life. Why are people even supposed to work eight hours a day at foaming milk? It kills your soul. Your brain dies. It sucks the energy right out of you and when you come back home you can't do anything but watch porn. Or whatever trashy reality show they have on TV. And what's the deal with foamed milk anyway? Why can't people just drink their coffee without having some poor guy stand for hours to foam it and then draw stupid pictures on top of it? What are they, three-year-olds?

I used to love my milk foamed when I still drank coffee or milk at all. But now my Ayurvedic nutritionist says milk makes me phlegmy so I've stopped with dairy altogether. No more cheese, butter, even yogurt. And I gave up bread too. And coffee, because I liked to drink it with a sweetener and that's poison. And no sugar, naturally, it's bad for you, even the brown kind. Lost three kilos in a month though, so that's cool.

How come you're drinking booze then?

I'm allowed to have wine and arak. Just no beer or whiskey or any other grain-based liquor, which is fine with me. I love arak. I also can't have tomatoes or cucumbers or eggplants or hummus...

That's, like, all the food there is! God, what do you eat?

All the rest, I guess. Pumpkin, carrot, green beans, barley, I don't know. Kasha. She says I'm kapha-pitta with too much vata, which is what makes me have my panic attacks. So I need to balance out the vata.

But I thought your panic attacks are related to war situations, no?

Yes. But the thing is that if I want to live here, you know, and not exile myself to some other place entirely, just live here in my homeland by the sea, in perfect weather, surrounded by my family and friends and all the countries around that don't recognise our right to be here–then I must find a way to cope with war-related stress.

And you think the way to do that is by balancing your Ayurvedic vata or whatever that is?

No, the vata is just one type, you see, we're all made of three types–kapha, pitta and—

OK, OK, let's not delve into that right now. With all my love and respect to India, and to you, I'm just not much into talking about New Age mumbo jumbo right now, OK? I say if you can't hold yourself from reading online news, which you know you shouldn't, and you find yourself panicking again because nobody helps the Syrians and you think they won't help us either when the day comes, which they won't, I assure you, or you make the huge mistake of watching TV news and you end up realising that Iran will evaporate us in one atomic split, to the sincere condolences of the West and the joyous rooftop dancing of the rest–just take Clonex. Really, it would do you much better than all that Ayurvedic bull.

Seriously, you don't know what you're talking about, Danny. First of all, it's not New Age at all, it's an ancient—

No, you know what, I just don't want to hear about it.

Let's just roll a joint and talk about my hate for customers, alright? Believe me, it's much healthier.

FRIDAY NIGHT AT AFRICA

So he says why don't you just take Clonex? To which I say, you do realise that you're offering me a Western capitalistic solution to stress which is caused by the same Western system in the first place, the system which is now trying to push its expensive trademark pharmaceutical drugs into me, but outlaws the much better drugs that I could have grown myself, but no, those are only to be smuggled illegally by Bedouins in the south, whose homes are now being demolished by the same horrid system, which is just mind-blowing, it's just—

But wait, where is he now, Danny? Why didn't you bring him with you?

Because I'm telling you, Noa, it's not gonna work out with him! All we ever do is smoke pot and fuck, there's never a decent conversation, and he always talks about himself for hours but won't listen to one full sentence of mine, and even if he did, I miss Saleh. I don't know if I can fall in love with someone else now.

Saleh! Didn't hear that name for a while now! I thought it was over months ago.

It was. It is. I just had too much pot to smoke and too much arak to drink. No, Saleh's back to Haifa now. Looking for someone that he can say "habibti" to and she will truly understand. As if I can't understand "habibti". As if I can't mean it when I say "habibi". He just enjoys breaking hearts.

Jewish hearts.

Don't be mean, Dorit.

I'm mean, Noa? I'm mean? Remind me who said she pities Liat for marrying an African refugee? Yes, Noa? Yes? Come on. Who's the racist?

Hey, I'm not a racist! It's not my fault you're all so PC it's like you were programmed at Microsoft. Let's face it–it's a hard life to be married to someone far less educated than you, who comes from a completely different culture, who's all alone here, while you are surrounded by your family and friends. Dorit, come on, remember yourself all alone in NY? Remember being stopped at the airport every single time because of your skin colour? Imagine that, times a hundred, everywhere, and that's Liat's husband's life here. They may have the cutest son ever, but it's terribly not easy.

Hell, I remember myself as a kid in London, when we lived there for a year so my dad could study laparoscopy, it was cutting-edge surgery back then in the early Eighties, but people in the shops would treat my mother like she's retarded. They would sometimes ignore her altogether or patronise her awfully simply because of her accent and foreign looks. I was just barely seven and I hated them. But really, all people everywhere are condescending pricks. That's why it's always better to live in your own homeland and be strong enough to take care of your own people, because nobody else will give a shit.

Hail to that! To the fatherland!

Oh, come on Rana, you know exactly what I mean. Don't turn on me now just because I'm saying the truth. You and Noa, you two privileged Ashkenazi white girls who grew up in the north of Tel Aviv, you're the last ones who should ever talk about liberal shit. You didn't grow up as the daughters of immigrants from Arab countries in an Eastern European version of a working utopia. You had it good in your nice liberal socialistic schools and your clean white secular neighbourhoods. It's all fun and nice and goody to believe in the kindness of strangers until you have to actually live with them or be them. Believe me, the majority of people who leave their homeland, whether as refugees or work immigrants or just because they want to try to live in another place, are lonely and homesick. It's hard to make new friends and succeed in a new language. That's what I think. And if you're gonna say that most people in the modern urban cities are just that anyway–lonely and homesick–then it just doesn't make it any better in my view. It's a fault, not an achievement. It shows we did something wrong.

OK, Dorit, we're with you. We hear you. We love you. We'll never desert you! Even if we are all of us refugees one day, after the bomb, we shall stick by you and give you a homey feeling wherever you go. To the camps of the future! Because no people has suffered enough, least of all the Persian Jews.

Great, Noa. But really.

No, really. Really. I love you.

Hey, me too! I love you Dorit. And you too, Noa. And I hope we can be three happy elderlies in the camps of the future. We'll take care of each other and never wear a bra even if our lives depended on it. The header at our camp's gate should say, in Persian wrought iron–*Love frees you*. In your ancestors' honor, Dorit. And also because we love the Iranians, except the very religious ones, and we wish all sides would dismantle their bombs. To Persian love! To love's labour camps! To the Labour Party!

Oh, God. I'm defeated. I love you all back, OK? My little drunk campy girlfriends. Now who's up for another round of arak?

Me!

Me!

Sababa, ya habibties. Back in a bit. Don't hit on any men, foreign or local, without me.

SATURDAY, VERY EARLY MORNING, OUTSIDE THE BLOCK

God, you're a great kisser.

You're not too bad yourself.

I won't normally ever start kissing a girl dancing next to me unless I'm totally shitfaced, you know.

I know. I can see you're British.

Scottish.

Oh, I'm sorry, I don't really follow the news anymore, I didn't know they…

No, they didn't, that's not what, oh–oh, that was nice.

It was.

Should we get a cab?

We can take a sherut, it goes all the way.

Let's go all the way then.

Funny Scot. Don't make promises you're too shitfaced to keep.

Haha. Don't worry, love. You ain't seen nothing yet.

So show me.

I will.

Oh, that wasn't bad at all.

No, it wasn't.

Can I teach you a word? Habibti.

Habibti, sounds like phlegm.

It does. That's funny. Perhaps we should stop saying that. Here, let's get on this one.

No, but it's a nice word, I like it. Habibti. What does it mean?

Can you pass our money? Twice, please. Thanks. It means, my love.

So where are you taking me, habibti?

Home, ya habibi. I'm taking you home.

THROUGH THE STORY OF THE GRID [1]

by Ronen Shamir

"The sun never sets on the British Empire," says Miss Lumley, tapping the roll-down map with her long wooden pointer. In countries that are not the British Empire, they cut out children's tongues, especially those of boys. Before the British Empire there were no railroads or postal services in India. And Africa was full of tribal warfare, with spears, and had no proper clothing. The Indians in Canada did not have the wheel or telephones, and ate the heart of their enemies in the heathenish belief that it would give them courage. The British Empire changed all that. It brought in electric lights.
—Margaret Atwood, *Cat's Eye*

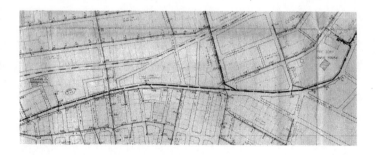

[1] © Materials are based on *Current Flow: The Electrification of Palestine*, Stanford University Press, 2013, by Ronen Shamir.

POWER STATION FROM SOUTH EAST

Among the various physical infrastructures around us, the electric grid is arguably the most critical for urban survival. Wherever we go, we see electric wires, streetlamps, and poles. They crawl under our feet, spring out of the ground, and cut across the sky above our heads. In fact, electric grids have become such a strong feature of life that they tend to disappear from view; we hardly notice them anymore. But here is an invitation: to follow electric wires, to walk the city along some of their routes, to discover some of their original logic and to uncover some hidden and forgotten aspect of the city.

In Mandate-day Palestine, wired electricity began in 1921 with a British concession to a Jewish entrepreneur by the name of Rutenberg who was licensed to produce and distribute electrical energy in the district of Jaffa (and, later, in the whole of Palestine). Herbert Samuel, the first British High Commissioner for Palestine (after whom the Tel Aviv beachfront promenade is still named), enthusiastically supported the concession and Winston Churchill, in charge of the British Colonial Office in London, put his political clout behind it as well.

At the time, Tel Aviv was just a modest middle-class neighbourhood next to bustling Jaffa. Almost all commercial activities took place in Jaffa and many neighbourhoods consisted of Arabs and Jews living side by side; in fact, the municipal borders between Jaffa and Tel Aviv were far from being firmly established and even when they were, they hardly reflected a strict ethnic division. The "business plan" of the Jaffa Electric Company that Rutenberg established had been to contract the Municipality of Jaffa and the local Council of Tel Aviv. Both bodies, each for its own population, were expected to buy electricity for water supply and streetlights. In this way, the company would also be able to branch off from this grid of electric distribution to individual residences and shops.

And so it was that the Jaffa Electric Company decided to build its electric powerhouse (producing electricity by means of diesel engines) in a neutral place between Jaffa and Tel Aviv. The work had begun in 1921. The architectural design of the powerhouse followed the latest hi-tech blueprints of Europe and the impressive building–for many years now deactivated as an electrical station–remains intact today.

Yet what was once a remote area is today one of Tel Aviv's most trendy areas. It is located in Ha'chashmal (literally "Electricity") Street. Right next to it are small coffee-houses and neighbourhood restaurants, as well as an array of small designer shops. Buildings in the neighbourhood are rapidly being gentrified, and just walking around, it is possible to get a good sense of the city's blend of "old" (well, almost one hundred years old!) and new. Right across from the powerhouse, crossing the busy Begin Road, is a completely different type of area: locally known as the "old central [bus] station", today it is home to documented and undocumented migrant workers from all over Africa, South America and south-east Asia, giving the area a very special (if controversial) character. It is highly recommended to walk around the area and experience a part of the city which is regrettably hardly frequented by visitors these days.

And then follow the wires. In tandem with the construction of the powerhouse, electrical works had also begun. The German electrical firm AEG supplied the machinery and the expertise. German engineers came to Jaffa to oversee the works, and the electric company opened a liaison office in Berlin. One of the notable features of the newly built grid was that the high-tension line that started at the powerhouse ran more or less parallel to the old Ottoman railway line connecting Jaffa and Jerusalem (see the essay on Lydda Junction in this book). Moreover, this high-tension line physically and visibly drew a boundary between Jaffa and Tel Aviv (see original map above). Although fed from the same source, the low-tension wires and poles that branched from the central high-tension line in the direction of Jaffa received their own serial numbers and constituted the grid "of Jaffa"; and the low-tension wires and poles that branched from the central high-tension line in the direction of Tel Aviv received their separate serial numbers and constituted the grid "of Tel Aviv".

You can still go down this central line today. Just walk from the powerhouse down Jaffa Road. Facing west, on your right will be Allenby Street (named after the British army general who led the conquest of Palestine in World War I) and Nachlat Binyamin Street. These were the first two streets that were ceremoniously lighted in June 1923. A bit further down on your left is the Levinsky Market area, strewn with some of the city's best delicatessen shops, spice and nut places, cafés and small tapas-like bars. A bit further to the south lies the neighbourhood of Florentin, home to many artists, street art wannabes, hipsters and all sorts of alternative lifestyle types. But you are digressing from the electric line by now. So, head back to Jaffa Road and, walking west, it soon becomes Eilat Street. Now you are approaching Jaffa. The reconstructed old train station will be on your right. You would be better avoid it if you prefer to stay away from tourist traps. Your route, following the wires, will soon bring you to Sderot Yerushalayim (Jerusalem Boulevard). Its original name was Jamal Pasha Boulevard, built by the modernising Ottoman ruler of Jaffa. After the British conquest, it was renamed King George

Boulevard. After the 1948 Jewish occupation of Jaffa, it got its present name.

In November 1923, the boulevard also ceremonially got its first dose of wired electric light. The Jaffa Electric Company located a transformer on the boulevard, where electric current from the high-tension line was transformed into low-voltage. This peculiar structure is still there as well, right where you are on the crossing of the Boulevard with Eilat Street. Comparing the photograph below (as well as that of the power station above) to the current landscape allows you a first-hand appreciation of the tremendous changes that has taken place here over the last eighty years.

So by now you can tell, just by having followed the wires, how the grid took an active part in the process of dividing the area into what eventually became two separate and often hostile towns—one Arab, one Jewish; a process that sadly culminated in the elimination of Jaffa as a significant Arab-populated city in 1948.

Transformer No.4.   King George V. Avenue, Jaffa.

THE UNDERSHIRT

by Shahar Shalev

It's hard to walk around Tel Aviv in the summer and not notice that a lot of men are wearing sleeveless undershirts–and not only to the beach. On central arteries, in the bars and clubs, in the shops and show windows–the masculine undershirt has a prominent place in the local wardrobe, perhaps more than any other fashion item.

The history of this garment is connected to pioneering anti-fashionability, simplicity and masculinity–all of which might serve to explain, in a paradoxical manner, its current appeal. Later, those characteristics worked their way into international trends, and the undershirt became one of the items beloved of local gay men. As they celebrate the liberation of the male body, it has become their ultimate fashion symbol.

What caused the undershirt to come out of the local closet here more than it has anywhere else in the world? Why do gay men see it as a desirable item? And can its story teach us something about the hidden connection between the male body, the Zionist project and local slovenliness, a connection we hadn't known about before?

At the end of the nineteenth century, undershirts and underpants as we know them didn't exist. There were only undergarments resembling overalls with long sleeves, something similar to an infant's onesie. Only at the beginning of the twentieth century did these union suits, as they were known in the United States, divide into pants resembling long underwear bottoms–affectionately known here by the Yiddish word gatkes–and T-shirts with long sleeves.

The T-shirt proper was invented only in 1913 in the British and American navies, as undergarments evolved as part of a re-evaluation of the uniforms worn by sailors serving on ships. The idea was to leave sailors' arms free when they were busy with tasks on deck (previous garments did not allow this). Thus, the white T-shirt was born.

The shirt was adopted immediately, since it was easy to see stains and dirt on it and thus maintain strict military hygiene, but it was still made of wool and other fabrics that are tough to get dry, and not particularly comfortable. Then companies like the British Sunspel (which has recently opened a new store in New York) and the American Fruit of the Loom developed and began manufacturing T-shirts from cotton, a move that made their shirts more popular, but still seen as an undergarment.

An early advertisement exhorted, "You don't need to be in the army to have a T-shirt of your own"–an ad that made the direct connection between the shirt and its military context, but at least until the end of World War II it was not considered legitimate to wear it without a top-shirt.

Or, in fact, at least not until Marlon Brando came along. Then, in the Fifties, the real revolution began and the T-shirt became a symbol of youth rebellion with all the sexy implications dripping from it, thanks to Brando in *A Streetcar Named Desire*, James Dean and jazz trumpeter Chet Baker, who wore it at every opportunity.

Only in the Seventies, with the flourishing culture of discotheques, drugs and the gay body cult, did the sleeveless undershirt–which eventually became known as the tank top–succeed in coming out of the closet and being displayed to the public in a context not connected to sports. In those years, men began to spend more and more time at gyms developing muscular bodies to show off, and the tank top became the ultimate garment that maximised the physical potential of its wearer.

The packed discotheques, with the energising drugs and sex that flourished in them, required minimal clothing, and the tank top was discovered to be a garment that revealed the male torso, from the arm muscles to the chest muscles. It was then that gay culture began to use the tank top as a sex symbol–a garment that, like jeans and the flannel shirt, had signified anti-fashion and the dripping masculinity that rejects preening and decoration.

Artists like Tom of Finland began to inundate the world with their gay pornographic paintings centred on cowboys, labourers and military men in torn jeans, boots, and tight, nearly bursting T-shirts or undershirts–and the undershirt became the gay popular front.

From there it moved into the male mainstream, thanks to Calvin Klein in the Eighties and Nineties, and fashion photographer Herb Ritts, who shot film actor Richard Gere in jeans and a white undershirt by a car in a garage. And a wealth of other icons in undershirts from the worlds of music and film–from Queen's Freddie Mercury to Brad Pitt in *Fight Club*–loaded patches of sweat and drool from gals and guys around the globe.

Surprisingly, however, the Israeli plain white undershirt came out of the closet way before all the rest. Maybe this was connected to the absence of proper dress rules, or maybe the perplexing mix of socialism and the pioneering ethos that built the foundations of fashion culture here–but the white undershirt had already been transformed from underwear to a symbol of the working proletariat back in the early days of the state.

During the years of the austerity regime, a decision was made to ration clothing items and shoes. In the annual allocation of ration coupons, relates Ayala Raz in her book *Changing Styles: 100 Years of Fashion in Eretz-Israel*, men were able to buy a woollen jacket, khaki shorts, a khaki shirt, a pair of cotton socks and two (!) undershirts, one for winter and one for summer—which marked the item out as the bread and butter of the local man.

At that time, the undershirt became fixed as the ultimate garment of the Zionist body: an item of clothing that expressed the muscular body, the grime of the labourer; the absence of decoration and elegance; something that rejected the fashionable bourgeoisie and celebrated Zionist labour and the pioneer beneath it.

Along with the uniform under which it peeked out or on its own, the men of Tel Aviv wore their undershirt and ate watermelon on the balconies of their homes, and the Israeli summer sanctified it on the way to the beach—thus, the undershirt became the unofficial male uniform, a minimal item for the maximal man.

LYDDA JUNCTION:
A TRAIN RIDE TO THE PAST [1]

by Ronan Shamir

"Night Train to Cairo" is a popular and highly recognisable 1980s Hebrew song by the legendary rock band Mashina. Its lyrics are about a fantasy trip, a badly needed getaway, or better still a hideaway. It is also a strong reminder of bygone days. Imagine Tel Aviv, Palestine, back in, say, the Thirties. The weekend is just around the corner and a friend suggests we spend it in Cairo. It should be fun and, moreover, simple to reach. We pack up lightly and walk south along the beachfront, approaching the towering mosques and churches of Jaffa a couple of miles ahead. Soon we have to turn left, walking down the road that leads to the Jaffa railway station. The train is about to leave for Jerusalem, but we only need a ticket for the shorter ride to Lydda Junction down its route. Once there we move from Platform 1 to Platform 3, catching the train to Kantara, via Gaza Strip, and from there to Cairo. On the platform, we come across the women in the photograph on the opposite page.

The women, posing for a farewell photo, are on their way to Cairo too. They are part of a formal delegation to Egypt, and they are proud and excited. Some of them

---

[1] © Materials are based on *Current Flow: The Electrification of Palestine*, Stanford University Press, 2013, by Ronen Shamir.

are traditionally dressed, some are showing off the latest European fashion; most are on high heels, while others have their heads properly covered. A British soldier is on guard, tensed; and yet the atmosphere is relaxed, even festive. This is the Middle East as it has been, or better still, as it still can be. A Holy Land that knows no borders.

This is not the Thirties. Yet the town of Lydda, for years downtrodden, forgotten, hardly on its feet, is still there. A fourteen-minute train ride and twelve-and-a-half shekels (roughly £2) are what it takes to reach the once glorious Lydda Junction railway station from the present-day Savidor Central railway station in Tel Aviv. Fourteen minutes, and a half-day excursion, allows one to step onto the platform–still the same one–that sustained late nineteenth-century Christian pilgrims to Jerusalem, Jaffa merchants on their way to the markets of Damascus, Palestinian dignitaries en route to Cairo, British soldiers who were stationed all over the land, or plain fun-seekers heading for a weekend in Cairo or Beirut.

"Hardly anyone remembers Lydda Junction these days," despairs the station master on a late Friday afternoon, and still "this is the heart of the country". Geographically speaking, he is right. When one looks around, with sharper eyes these days, it is possible to appreciate that it is still a major hub: multiple rails, parked locomotives, and quite a few cargo and passenger trains speeding through every few minutes. But, paradoxically, the distances it is possible to travel from Lydda Junction today have shrunk considerably since the Thirties and Forties. Rather than Cairo or Damascus, Beersheba–one hour away–or Nahariya, roughly two hours away–are the most once can hope for these days. Inaccessible borders and derelict lines prevent longer distances.

The original terminal building is still there, almost intact. "We saved it from total destruction," says the station master. Yet it is poorly maintained and latter-day additions hardly respect its old days of glory. The story of Lydda Junction goes back to the later years of the nineteenth century, when the Ottoman rulers of Palestine became eager to modernise the country. They licensed a French company to build and run a railway line from Jaffa to Jerusalem. Jaffa was the main sea port of the country, for hundreds of years the launching pad to the holy city of Jerusalem, roughly sixty kilometres to the east. As it were, the east-west line between the two cities also ran through the middle of the country, marking its northern from its southern hemisphere. And Lydda, a modest Palestinian village next to the bigger and more glorious town of Ramlah, was located roughly midway on the Jaffa-Jerusalem railway line. The British army–occupying Palestine in 1917–had been quick to realise the strategic importance of the place. Lydda Junction was the point where the Jaffa-Jerusalem Railway line met the railway line that came all the way from Cairo in the south, heading north through Kantara and Rafah (in the Gaza Strip). Soon it also became a junction for a line that headed north to Haifa and to an extension of the famous Hedjaz railway line that was to carry Muslim pilgrim from Damascus, through Trans-Jordan, all the way to Medina in present-day Saudi Arabia. The British were therefore quick to locate the army and air force headquarters nearby (Sarafand) and these very same military barracks are now home to many training centres of the Israeli army (Zrifin). The proximity to Lydda Junction is also the reason the British built the country's major airport nearby, appropriately named Lydda Airport. Today, this is the very same Ben Gurion International Airport.

No wonder that the accidental traveller meets a crisp

breeze of history on the Lydda Junction platform! Once there, take a loving look around, sort out the old from the recent, and fly your imagination to the past. When you have had enough, a small digression is highly recommended. Just two miles away, easily reached by foot or bus, lies the town of Ramlah with its old churches, bustling markets and superb restaurants. For Arab food lovers, the Halil restaurant is the princess and its masabacha (a fine version of hummus) is the jewel in the crown. People will send you to Abu Hassan in Jaffa, and you are most welcome to sample and compare, but absolutely nothing compares with the masabacha of Halil. So hop on a train, get a sense of the country's modestly hidden "heart", sense the neglect, imagine a better past and future, and treat yourself to a hearty meal before your return trip to reality. [2]

---

[2] For historical photographs see:
http://actsofminortreason.blogspot.co.il/2009/05/pdp-46-day-guard-at-lydda.html

Photograph by Ellen Levy-Arie

THE STORY OF THE SABICH (OR THE NEW FALAFEL)

by Ron Levy-Arie

What started out originally as a Saturday morning breakfast food of Iraqi Jews has become a sort of a national Israeli street food that has even cast a shadow over the well-known and much-loved falafel. The urban legend of the dish starts in the sleepy suburb of Ramat Gan back in 1961. A newcomer from Iraq opens up a small food stand in a neighbourhood by the name of Nahalat Yitzhak. The young man sells a simple sandwich he knows from back home. The ingredients are basic, yet compose a perfect combination for the mouths of No. 63 bus drivers on their way to their daily route. The clients used to call the owner by his first name, Sabich. They used to call at him, and say: "Make me a dish, Sabich!" (No "please" included, typical Israeli style.) Therefore the name of the dish was born. Others disapprove of this version, and claim that the dish had been familiar amongst Iraqis by that name because the word sounds similar to the Arab word "sabach", meaning "morning", and since it is a breakfast delight, it would make sense for this to be the true reason for the name. In Israel, even street food brings conflict.

The sandwich is made in pitta bread, includes slices of deep-fried aubergine, hard-boiled brown egg, tahini sauce, shredded onions and parsley, some finely chopped salad, homemade hot sauce and the secret ingredient, amba–a word in Arabic that originated from Sanskrit, meaning mango. This unique product made its way to Iraq due to the work of spice traders from India, who brought pickled mangoes to the Iraqis. They then mixed and diluted them with water and oil, and this sauce merged into Iraqi cuisine. It carries a strong fenugreek and allspice aroma that comes from an Iraqi spice blend known as baharat, which is also mixed into that special shining-yellow sauce. Some folks avoid including it in the sandwich due to the fact that the smell lingers with you throughout the day, and you can even smell it when you sweat. Yet it is still worth taking that risk.

Right until the late Nineties and early Noughties, falafel was the undisputed national street food. Usually Israel tends to "borrow" food invented by Arab countries and call it her own. From the Fifties onwards, falafel was the ultimate street food favourite, made by local Palestinians or by Jews coming from Egypt, Yemen or Syria. It was cheap and accessible and is made by the most lovable pea in the Middle East, the chickpea. The other key ingredient is hummus, which by itself stands as the ultimate dish of the Middle East.

Then the sabich started shining. The guy who popularized it the most is called Oved, and comes from the neighbouring town of Ramat Gan, Givatayim. Oved claims to make the best sabich dish in the universe, and even invented a sabich-based slang and a theatrical way of preparing the dish, in which he addresses the customer in the manner of an enthusiastic football announcer and questions them about their desired amount of toppings in a dialect that derives from the football fields. He created the craze, and after Israelis had been through the "Oved experience"–which also includes a DIY Hall of Fame of record-breakers in sabich-eating–others soon started opening sabich shops, such as the famous Sabich Frishman in Tel Aviv. Even old-time falafel stands added sabich to their falafel-based menus. The sabich of today is even served as a sandwich in posh cafés and restaurants, rising from rags to riches.

The "godfather of the sabich", the originator of the dish, kept selling it at the corner of Negba and Haroe, with his scanned ID hanging on the wall showing his first name. Sadly, this culinary genius passed away a couple of years back, but his sons continue their father's tradition and serve the dish with great pride.

INSOMNIA

by Ithamar Handelman-Smith
(published under the pen name Ithamar Ben Canaan,
translated by Shlomzion Kenan)

I walk into the Allenby 58 club with Oren Agmon. We get past the guest list bouncer and go straight down to the lower-deck lounge. Oren Agmon, my boss, runs into three of his college pals and they hit the dancefloor.

"I don't like this music," I yell into his ear. "I hate rap. I'm going upstairs."

"Are you going up?" Ivy, one of those 'pals' of his, is asking.

"I'll come with you," she continues. She's a medium-height girl with short black hair cut just below her ears. She's wearing black pants and there's some sort of black rag wrapped around her chest. "You remind me of Anaïs Nin—well, anyhow, of the actress who played her in that film—what was the name of it... about their life together, about Henry Miller and Anaïs Nin..."

"*Henry and June*," she says. "That must be on account of my being French. I have this French look."

We go upstairs to the dancefloor. She locks her arm into mine, and then yells, "Let's go dancing. I'm nuts about this song." I say, "Yes, 'Insomniac', that's a fine song."

"Inso-maniac," she giggles. "Inso-MANIAC."

In the background we hear the line, "I can't get no sleep," then it hits off. The music elevates, higher and higher until everyone's hands are up in the air, glasses are breaking and people are screaming and then...74boom, boom.... The bass kicks in, the beat picks up and I fix my gaze at her dancing.

"Aren't you dancing?"

"What? I can't hear you."

"Aren't you dancing?" she asks again, her slim arms batting in the air and her pelvis twisting and whirling about.

"No, no," I say, "I'm too blasted. I had four hits just before I got here and a couple of drinks." She takes hold of me, her hands grabbing my arms at the elbows, her head draws near, her lips press against mine and we kiss.

"Let's go upstairs," she says.

We go up to the gallery. I pull her to the far-left corner, under the top bar staircase. We go through a black curtain and kiss. She unties the knot off that rag that's wrapped around her, and I undo her bra that opens up front. Her breasts are pretty small, with dark, erect nipples. I lick her and her hand glides down my pants and into my underwear and she jerks me off. With her free hand she pushes my fingers into her cunt, which is, by now, totally wet. I feel her pussy, play with her clitoris, and insert my fingers into her. I start with one finger, then two, three and finally four.

"Wow... wow..." she moans. Then she gives a faint sigh and comes.

"Let's go to your place," I say.

"Yeah," she says. "Let's go."

It's raining outside. We catch a cab and drive up to her place on Weizmann Street. All the way there, in the back seat of the cab, she has her left hand in my pants, jerking me off. The cab pulls over in front of her building and I pay up. The stony path that leads to her front door is covered with overhead shrubbery. When she's halfway across, she stops.

"I have a boyfriend," she says. "This doesn't feel right."

"So you want me to leave?"

"No, no," she says. "That's the problem. I need you to fuck me."

We go into her apartment, on the first floor. We undress and get into bed. She blows me and I give her head and then penetrate her. The first time is over pretty quickly. The second time lasts longer, we do it doggy style.

We smoke a cigarette and I hold her. She strokes my cock.

"I've never had anything like this. You see, I was a virgin 'til twenty. Then, for three-and-a-half years since my first time, I couldn't stop fucking. I just love sex. But with you... you're something else... it's as though... almost like losing my virginity all over again. I'd like you to come and fuck me all the time. Just call me, come over, fuck me and leave. That's all I want. I just... wow... I can't get over this cock of yours." I take another puff off my cigarette and say nothing.

"Pity you have so many tattoos though. I don't care for that at all. Such a nice body, why cover it up with silly cartoons..."

"But you said you loved my cock."

"Oh yes, I'm crazy about your cock, that's one hell of a penis you've got there between your legs, mister, the largest by far I ever had," she says, and proceeds to suck on it again. She's licking my balls and my arsehole. I don't respond.

"Fine, we'll carry on next time," she says. "But you will come, won't you? Listen, I won't freak out on you. I have a boyfriend and I love him, but how can I make love to him now that I've developed a taste for your amazing penis? So just drop by and fuck me. Whenever you feel like it. I will always spread my legs for your exceptional cock."

"So you want me to come and fuck you whenever I feel like it?"

"Yes," Ivy says. "Come over, fuck me, fuck me as much as you like and leave, and now," she says, "I'm going to get some sleep."

I get off the bed and put my suit on. The tie has whiskey stains on it and the knot is loose. Ivy scribbles her phone number on a flyer I was handed at Allenby 58, an invitation to hear DJ Brandon Block, who'll be playing the club the following Thursday night.

"I bet you won't call."

"I'll call you," I say.

"Call me," she says. "I'll be waiting right here, legs wide apart. Call, come over, fuck me, then leave."

We kiss and I go. Before leaving the apartment I rinse my hands in the sink. I go out to the street. It's a quarter before six and the sky is luminous. I walk past a green garbage can. I pause, take out the invite to Thursday night's party featuring Brandon Block on the turntables, the flyer with Ivy's number scribbled on it with a blue Parker pen. I hold it out briefly and then toss it into the garbage can. I keep walking towards Judas Maccabi Street. When I hit Judas Maccabi I turn left and walk down the street until it intersects with Ibn Gabirol. I wait for a bus, the 48, which will take me to my folks' house in Herzelia. I smoke my last cigarette, which I drew out of a crushed pack and straightened out a little. I sniff the tips of my fingers; they still give out her scent. At twenty past six I get on the bus and sit next to a Thai construction worker. I stir nervously in my seat. It seems as though everyone in the bus can smell the odour that's emanating from me, the cunt aroma of Ivy or Shmivy or whatever her name was, the smell of her cunt that's oozing from my fingers.

PART TWO: KEDMA

(Translates both as "east" and as "progress" or "forward-facing", as the ancient Israelites looked at the east instead of today's north. Alshrq in Arabic)

BEULAH LAND: THE LINE BETWEEN THE TWO WORLDS (THE BLUES AND THE PROMISED LAND)

by Eran Sebbag (Translated by Eilam Wolman)

On Maxwell Street Market in Chicago, Illinois, childhood haunt of brothers Leonard and Phil Chess, who later formed the Chess Records label, a legendary graffiti on a wall reads: "Blacks + Jews = Blues." Maxwell Street is the cradle of Chicago blues. The inscription was there before the eyes of all who passed.

These words referred to the historical link between Blacks and the Jewish children of European immigrants who went into the business of recording, producing and marketing blues music. The following essay isn't concerned with the logistics of this musical collaboration, but with the inherent connections between the Jews and the bluesmen. At first, this relation may seem curious, perhaps even illogical: what do the Jews of Europe have to do with African-American music from the Mississippi Delta? Few Jews settled in the South and the Mississippi Blacks who reached the shtetls of Podolia were quite scarce to say the least. Our concern is the connection that many Jews felt to Black music–music rooted in the chain gang, born in the struggle for freedom. To understand the unlikely yet deep connection between Jewish thought (especially movements such as

Hasidism[1] and ancient mysticism) and the gospel of the blues, we must explore the two doctrines' common root.

The blues originated in the Mississippi Delta. We don't know who the first person to sing the blues was, and probably never will, but what cannot be denied is that the woeful chant which arose from slavery and bondage created a canon that transcended the miserable historic and material circumstances of its formation. Its object being simply the human struggle of one's soul, the blues became a universal song of comfort and solidarity. Whether this was the direct intention of the blues or simply how it came to be received is irrelevant. What is important is that the blues was an existential rebellion of the exploited and enslaved, speaking to universal feelings of persecution. As Mississippi Fred McDowell put it in the short lines of his song "You Got to Move", a practical anthem distilling the deep existential gospel of the Blues:

> You may be high
> You may be low
> You may be rich, child
> You may be po'
> But when the Lord gets ready
> You got to move

---

[1] Hasidism (or Hasidic Judaism), derives from the Hebrew word "hesed", meaning "piety" or "loving kindness", and is a large branch of the Jewish ultra-orthodoxy that was founded in mid-eighteenth-century Ukraine by rabbi Israel (Yisroel) Baal Shem Tov, who placed emphasis on a popular and common version of kabbalah (Jewish mysticism) and the joy and happiness in worshiping Hashem (God) rather than just learning the Talmud and the Torah in the strict and academic manner of the Lithuanian branch of ultra-orthodoxy.

Mississippi Fred sums it up. The slave, the master, the wealthy and the destitute are one. As Ecclesiastes (the exemplary biblical book of the blues) states:

> What profit hath a man of all his labor which he taketh under the sun? One generation passeth away, and another generation cometh: but the earth abideth forever.

The bluesman understands that in the deepest sense–we are all slaves, all insignificant to the ruthless vagaries of the world.

Africans were brought to the New World in the most degrading way imaginable–taken captive, sold into slavery and boarded onto slave ships. Their identity was eradicated and they were rendered as nothing more than property. A hundred years after the abolition of slavery, the social state of African-Americans remained quite unchanged: segregation laws, the Ku Klux Klan, lynching, and blatant racism.

The African-American's static condition as a degraded and excluded individual fomented an unwavering perception of man's fate. Though rooted in this social context, the blues offered relief for any predicament the living soul encounters in the world. It is perhaps because of this that the blues is usually composed in the present tense. Even when there is a reference to the past, it is the immediate past ("Woke up this mornin'"), and the undefined future in the blues mostly goes only as far as a few moments from the present time ("I'm going, don't know where I'm going but I'm going"). This song of the present teaches us that "the thing that hath been, it is that which shall be" and that it is futile to imagine anything "new under the sun".

The Jew in exile and the enslaved African-American share a marginalised status and a common experience of insistent persecution and oppression. They were both concerned with their everyday lives and did not aspire to change the world or envision a different future.

Just as Jewish and Hasidic spiritualism provided a critique of the "old" institutionalised religion, the blues transcended the churches and houses of worship in the South. Religion offers its believers redemption and guarantees that every believer will receive his reward in the next world. Yet the bluesman and the mystic understand that man's business and heavy load are matters of this world, and that we do not live for the future but for today.

The blues did move beyond the church and venture into the expanses of life in the painful present, but it did not forget its religious roots, transposing religion's terms into symbols man can use in everyday life. The blues never separated from the gospel, and the gospel retained a tacit critique of the white Christian establishment.

Taking biblical events and terms from the Old Testament can be seen as a rebellion against the new one. Many blues texts resonate with the Jew, who from time immemorial has struggled to survive in exile, and who uses the same concepts put forth in the blues to describe his own redemption. The slaves undoubtedly saw themselves as the children of Israel enslaved in Egypt and used the narrative of the Old Testament to describe their plight. The white master is seen as Pharaoh and the segregated South is Egypt. The land of Israel–or in the language of the blues, the Promised Land–is the place where one could live fearlessly, where there is no lynching and no subservience. Accordingly, the Jordan River is not only the river itself, but also the line between the two worlds. This one and the next. Good and evil. The chains and unattainable freedom. The historic root is identical in both cases and was used in the folk singing which developed later as well. For the Jew of the diaspora, there was also the material concept of the land of Israel, the Jordan River, Jerusalem, etc., although, as he spent generations in exile, the land of Israel and its regions became internal concepts, a guiding and comforting ideal in a chaotic world. Hence, it emerges that for the Jew hearing the blues for the first time in his life, not only the religious concepts but the geography itself was familiar. The blues can be considered the non-Jewish tradition closest to the essence of Jewish spiritualism and of the Hasidic faith, which also broke through the confines of its religious establishment.

Mississippi bluesman John Hurt sings: "I got a mother in Beulah Land outside the sun / Way beyond the sky."

"Beulah Land", a married land, refers to the land whose sons returns to and unite with, just like the union between man and woman. This hymn derives from the King James version of Isaiah 62:4: "Thou shalt no more be termed Forsaken; neither shall thy land any more be termed Desolate; but thou shalt be called *Hephzibah* and thy land *Beulah*; for the LORD delighteth in thee, and thy land shall be married." The verse is in reference to the return of the Jews from their exile in Babylon, in which the Jews shall no longer be called *Forsaken*, but *Hephzibah* (My Delight Is in Her), and Jerusalem shall no longer be called *Desolate*, but *Beulah* (Married). This implies that the Jews have turned back to the worship of God.

In this case, it is the English-speaking bluesman who lacks the necessary Hebrew to get to the bottom of the term. Beulah means a land that has been cultivated by its inhabitants—which is to say, be fruitful and multiply, and the land will provide.

There is no shortage of such examples. The Hebrew language, the geography of the land of Israel, the biblical heroes, and above all, an unrevealed shared fate of the Blacks and Jews, exist both in the gospel and later in the blues. Both traditions share the hope for survival and peace of mind in a material world of pain.

IN MY HEART
by Reuven Miran
(Translated by Eilam Wolman)

One warm morning in early July, Ella Fitzgerald and I drove
from Kfar Saba to Jerusalem. We started driving east, and
then we turned south, then east again. The sun was still
low and it stung my eyes intermittently. From south of
Rosh HaAyin, we entered a dusty boulevard of carob trees.
Crushed scraps piled among the dry branches. Washers,
baking and cooking ovens, broken and crinkled plastic
and aluminium blinds, which once concealed many things.
The east wasn't far. Dust rose from the direction of the
quarries that suddenly blocked the eastern horizon. Migdal
Afek–or Mirabel Fortress, depending on the period and
circumstances–seemed abandoned. We drove up there for a
moment without leaving the car. A single word was smeared
in thick black on one of the thick external walls–Palestine.
The once-black soot of bonfires now grayed upon the stones.

We came down and continued, driving by the olive and fig
trees haphazardly scattered on the hills, between the rocks
whose grey heads alone glanced through the thorns. The
thorns were dry. Tall, thin cypresses grew between them.
One spark, I thought, one spark is all it would take.

In Bayt Nabala junction we saw burnt eucalyptuses.
What was left of their leaves was yellow and grey. Scorched
branches were growing from the sooty trunks. Not far, next

to a stop sign, stood a boy with a stroller which was once green and now carried a large pile of pretzels. A brown military truck passed him and stopped for two seconds, because of the sign. The road was empty. Bright, thin dust ascended from its double back wheels.

We stopped close to him. Ella stayed in the Subaru. I got off. The shift stick was in the dead zone. The engine kept running. The air was cool and pleasant. A light wind brought it to us from the west.

"Small pretzel for a shekel and a half, a big one for two," said the boy.

He was an Arab boy with yellow hair and big, blue eyes, like the sky enfolding the entire land. The dust on his tall forehead mixed with sweat and their composite was slowly dripping behind his earlobes.

"Two big ones," I said. One for me and one for Ella, I thought. The scent of baked dough and singed sesame hit my salivary glands. The boy inserted two big pretzels into a transparent black nylon bag. Afterwards he threw some za'atar in the bag from a yellow page torn from an old phone book.

As soon as I opened the car door, I heard Ella again. The pretzels were warm. Their tender scent filled the tight space. We ate driving between the fields of cotton, corn and vine. An old Boeing 707 clambered westward slowly and noisily, the sun blazing on its tail. I was silent, so I could hear Ella better.

Before the unsignposted left turn to Kfar Truman, she said: "I always knew / I would live my life through / with a song on my lips for you."

I wasn't sure and I also don't remember if it was "with a song on my lips" or "with a song in my heart", and I didn't care too much, at least not at that moment. The big band

Photographs by Assaf Shoshan (originally in colour)

Photograph by Assaf Shoshan (originally in colour)

accompanying her was fighting with the constant rattle of the engine. Together they overpowered my eardrum, and I didn't exactly hear the words woven in her big, warm voice.

Ella didn't make it all the way to Jerusalem with me. I bade her farewell at Sha'ar HaGai and she might have moved to a different driver on a different station. I continued alone among the pastel pines and cypresses. The armoured vehicles, painted with anti-rust primer, were there as usual, the withered flower bouquets from a previous ceremony laid on them. The sky was blue like the large eyes of the boy whose pretzels' scent still stood in the car. Something suffocated me from inside. I thought after Motza the air would be chillier and easier to breathe. But it was hot and heavier and it sat deep in my chest. I turned on the AC. A brisk gust filled the car and opened up my lungs at once. I drove slowly. In the side mirror, I saw a truck cutting me without hesitation. It had a blue license plate from the territories and it was full of empty Coca-Cola bottles. It disappeared behind the curve and I was alone again.

Suddenly I remembered. "In my heart," she said. I was sure of it now. In my heart.

TECHNICOLOUR IN JERUSALEM
by Tom Shoval (Translated by Eilam Wolman)

I'm a cinephile. Cinema is like a religion to me. This means that my life is divided into two spheres: reality, which I find comparatively interesting; and reality's mirror image, cinema, where I would rather live. Aware of the impossibility of living inside movies, I search for archaeological findings, evidence on the ground that cinema was here, next to me. By unearthing the dinosaur tracks of cinema, I prove that reality and magic did in fact intersect. Of course, from the prism of reality, it looks like I'm only collecting memorabilia from past films and nothing more. It's a matter of perspective, but also one of principle.

The trouble with being a cinephile and living in Israel is the dearth of findings. Israeli cinema is indeed maturing, but its past, though solid, lacks in sensational revelations. Cinema flourishes in other continents, in the Hollywood climate, or as a reflection of the subtle European light. Israel is an historical and Archimedean site, but for cinema it is a land not sown. With the basalt stones and the stark light disfiguring every frame, living up to the exciting portrayals of the land in the Hebrew Bible, the Quran and the New Testament is nearly impossible for a film. It's as though Israel were a trap laid for the very pretence to film it. Still, I don't despair, and continue my searches for a pivotal moment where cinema history took place in the country. Indeed, the

Lumière brothers were here and they shot a train leaving a station in Jerusalem. But that doesn't really count either; the Lumières were eminent globetrotters who shot trains leaving every station in every country. Doesn't count.

Seeking out every book I could find that might contain a nugget of information about such a cosmic convergence, I eventually came upon acclaimed cinematographer and director Jack Cardiff's book *Magic Hour* (Faber & Faber, 1996). Cardiff, one of the greatest cinematographers who ever lived, is most famous for the Technicolour nature shots he took in the films of Michael Powell and Emeric Pressburger–*The Red Shoes*, *The Tales of Hoffmann*, *A Matter of Life and Death*, *Black Narcissus*, and, of course, *The Life and Death of Colonel Blimp*. Cardiff's intricate artistry lent a new form to the fierce colours afforded by Technicolour and almost turned the frames in these films into moving paintings.

Technicolour is a method of developing film which allows for the containment of colour. The technique itself was invented in the first years of the previous century and continued to evolve, unleashing a fierce fabric of colours on celluloid as early as the late Twenties. One of the greatest moments in the history of cinema, the arrival of Dorothy in Oz in *The Wizard of Oz*, was shot in Technicolour, which was crucial for Oz's magical, glowing atmosphere. Hollywood couldn't resist the magic of Technicolour and it painted its films with its fierce, saturated pigments. Cinema was like a fresh bouquet of flowers in those days. Director Francis Ford Coppola famously said that Technicolour has babied cinema. In 1932, the elders of the Technicolour community developed a special camera that would film in Technicolour so the colour wouldn't have to be injected or processed in a laboratory. The camera they produced was as innovative as it was unwieldy. In addition to the bulky camera, Technicolour film required plenty of light and a special exposure, and getting good results from it wasn't easy for cinematographers.

Around that time, a German count by the name of von Keller and his wife came to the offices of Kay Harrison, managing director of Technicolour in the UK. They wanted to hire a Technicolour camera and a cameraman to shoot travelogues around the world. Harrison tried to explain that the cumbrous camera required constant maintenance. The wealthy von Kellers kept insisting, and eventually they had their way. The Technicolour camera's results impressed von Keller to such a degree that it became his mission to prove to the film world that the device was invulnerable to any production mishap and could deliver excellent results in any condition and under any exposure. He needed a cinematographer who would be willing to embark on such an adventure as would convince everyone that the Technicolour camera was the next big thing.

Jack Cardiff had already shot a few films in Technicolour, and he was a master at producing beautiful frames with speed and little effort. He had a flair for adventure and he took the offer immediately. Von Keller sought to re-accomplish the Lumière brothers' achievement and shoot all over the world with the Technicolour camera. He wanted to create a "second take" of the Lumière Brothers' act of cinematic wonder. As they had made the audience flee the theatre for the fear that the train would burst from the screen and run them over, von Keller believed he could make the audience see the beauty of the world's colours for the first time. Perhaps the name "cinema" would be replaced with the more mysterious "Technicolour". Cardiff found himself loading the awkward camera equipment onto a ship and sailing across the sea with the von Kellers and a limited crew to shoot a series of Technicolour shorts called *World Window*. Their second stop was Jerusalem.

When I read this, my jaw dropped. One of the first attempts at location shooting with the Technicolour camera happened in *Jerusalem*. Cardiff describes shooting in Jerusalem in great detail in his book. To me, his stories read like something out of Verne or Kipling, a British expedition's adventures in an unknown place–a modern excursion to the ancient Holy Land.

The year is 1937 and Palestine is under the rule of the British mandate. There are tensions towards the mandate from both Arabs and Jews. The crew docks in the port of Haifa, shoots around Mount Carmel and continues towards Jerusalem, which captivates Cardiff. He seems to have almost prepared himself in advance to experience the divine presence in the holy city, but amazingly and perhaps predictably for a cinematographer, he finds spirituality in the city's light, of all phenomena. Here is Cardiff from the book:

> There is something splendidly defiant about old Jerusalem. Walking through the narrow, dark, traffic-free lanes of the old quarter, one is magically transported to biblical times... the scene is wonderfully unchanged. Only my Technicolour camera was out of harmony, but the light was heavenly: shafts of sunlight, sharpened by the dust which penetrated shadowed air like golden swords.

Was it merely his foreign eye, eager for sanctity, that imagines these swords of light? Is it the colonial gaze of his time and place? Perhaps, but it's impossible to ignore Cardiff's genuine passion for the holy city and the urgency he felt to capture the light that falls over it.

Jack Cardiff, cameraman

Cardiff's awe is palpable in the slow pans with which he reveals the area, shooting through cracks in the walls and revealing bits of landscape struck by the fierce light. He shoots a deserted valley with broken basins that look as if they'd just been placed there. Some of the "natives", the narrator will testify in the final edit, still use them to carry water. A gorgeously coloured shot of a group of girls walking with heavy water basins on their heads will cut to a shot of Franciscan priests on their way to prayer.

Cardiff shot non-stop, and he relates how the residents were distracted by and drawn to the film crew, and especially to the massive Technicolour camera. Imagine this modern mammoth at the centre of an ancient quarter in 1937 Jerusalem, absorbing and immortalising the images of everyday life.

The camera performs a religious function, operating as a mythologising filter, manufacturing spirituality, or making a latent one explicit. Armed with his naked eye, Cardiff joyously and sensitively creates a new mythology.

The film reveals a spiritual world full of pathos and grandeur. The camera is in constant circular motion, shooting from low angles, grabbing bits of sky, revealing sacred areas where the past is still alive. The provisional is filtered out. Extras walk in exemplary order and silence with no outside interruptions. The *mise-en-scène* is standard, archaic yet breathtaking. Ever the professional, Cardiff deftly processes what's before his eyes while sketching outlines of the ghosts that might still wander the Via Dolorosa.

In the evenings, Cardiff presents a different Jerusalem, turbulent and modern. Ragtime at the King George Hotel. Cigars, women in lace dresses and men in frock suits, their hair slicked back with European gel. Dancing continues into the small hours of the morning. Cardiff marvels at the coexistence of the hallowed with the modern. With the muses singing and the night-time rousing his instincts, he doesn't imagine that this harmony might be only in his head.

Cardiff, the hunter of light, wants to shoot the walls of the Old City during the magic hour. The crew rushes to a steep hillock overlooking the city. Afraid to lose the valuable minutes of sunset, Cardiff quickly sets up the camera. Suddenly gunshots ring out. Bandits who, like anyone else in the Old City, couldn't help but notice the technological beast want to take the metal giant captive. The crew members look at each other, wondering whether to fold the camera that could take a bullet at any moment or perhaps save themselves first. Cardiff is concerned only with the completion of the shot he is taking, and as the gunshots escalate, he finishes the exposure process. He sends his crew to the car at once, takes the camera apart by himself and runs away with it. A bullet singes his shirt.

They drive north to Haifa. There, in a hotel room, Cardiff recounts the latest events to Count von Keller. After asking Cardiff to promptly send the rushes for development, von Keller telephones the British High Commissioner of Palestine and tells him about the film crew's run-in with the bandits. The concerned commissioner promises to look after the matter. The next morning, Cardiff is awoken by a phone call from a British officer who tells him the outlaws have been apprehended on the previous night and will be trialled. He asks to meet with Cardiff and pick up his testimony.

Cardiff meets the officer for breakfast on the terrace of the King George Hotel. They have a pleasant and intelligent conversation. The cinematographer is very impressed with the young officer. That same day, he boards a ship to meet his crew, which is already waiting for him in Damascus. Eventually, Cardiff realises that the young officer he'd met was the legendary Orde Charles Wingate, one of the originators of modern guerrilla warfare, whose unconventional ideas about organising guerrilla troops were successfully implemented in British campaigns and adopted by many corps. A devout Christian, Wingate was an ardent champion of Zionism and saw it as a moral and religious virtue to build the Jewish community in Palestine a state. He was crucial in training Haganah fighters, and his ideas provided the foundation for what was to become the Israel Defense Forces (IDF). Cardiff didn't only look to the past but also came across a man whose effect on the future of the place was immense. His Technicolour camera documented the empty alleyways where Jesus walked, and also illumined the conflicts that continue to fissure the land many generations later.

And so, another point of contact between the history of Israel and the history of cinema has been found. Allow me to note another interesting confluence in closing. In 1965, the great director Pier Paolo Pasolini arrived in Israel to scout for locations for a film he intended to make based on the New Testament, *The Gospel According to St Matthew* (1964). With a 16mm camera, Pasolini passes more or less through the same places in Israel that Cardiff had thirty years before. But Pasolini's impression couldn't be farther from Cardiff's. He finds no holiness in Israel to speak of. The land doesn't contain the open expanses which would allow for such holiness to emerge. He films his visit and makes a short documentary called *A Visit to Palestine* (1963). Did the years gone by and the founding of the state of Israel terminate the air of sanctity, or is it just the sharper, more critical and disenchanted gaze of a Marxist intellectual such as Pasolini? As always, history too is a matter of perspective.

Pier Paolo Pasolini and Tonino Delli Colli at work on Il Decameron

Pasolini in Palestine

FEAR AND LOATHING IN THE DEAD SEA

by Dan Shadur

The AC at the Golden Tulip Hotel can barely ward off the furnace outside. Tzachi, the photographer, is staring at a large mosaic in the lobby. It's supposed to be a depiction of some biblical episode, calling to mind archaeological findings from the area. I'm calling Shiri, the PR woman, who isn't picking up. The night before, I got an urgent call from the editor of the paper I work for. He found out that Leonora Souza, one of his favourite South American actresses—he's obsessed with telenovelas, don't ask me—is shooting a campaign for an Israeli cosmetics company with plants in occupied Palestinian territories, and he thought it would be interesting to send his political reporter on her trail. Since it was too late to book an interview, he gave me the PR woman's number and said if I come back without a story he's "hanging me from the balls in the middle of the newsroom". Shimi Goldberg sometimes liked to pretend he was a tough American actor in a political thriller set in a newspaper building. It was almost as equally effective as it was ridiculous.

I picked Tzachi up from his apartment in Tel Aviv. We eventually reached Sodom Arad Road, winding along a variety of rocks in changing shades down to the Dead Sea, possibly the most beautiful drive in Israel. Tzachi wasn't the greatest photographer in the annals of Israeli media, but his fondness for drugs and unusual experiences helped kill the dead hours between tasks and increased the likelihood of something interesting happening. He would also take laborious portraits of the writers he worked with that we could frame and be proud of, which made us all forgive him for the many photo ops he had botched. Now he's extracting his camera, unable to take a single picture. I think he's experiencing artistic castration anxiety in the face of the stunning, lunar-looking scenery; the sun glistening in the black basalt and white chalk and countless shades of brown and red, until the glittering blue of the sea emerges from beyond the road. Without saying anything, I stop the car at one of the lookout points and we leave the AC for the arid furnace. Somebody stuck an ugly pirate memorial here for a loved one who died in a horrifying motorcycle accident. We smoke a joint and gaze into the horizon. In the summer, this is one of the hottest places in the world. In the winter, the weather here is perfect. Behind us, the arresting desert rocks are changing with the light. Before us lie the endless mountains of Jordan and the sea. Where is Leonora Souza right now and what is she doing? Does she know we're coming to look for her?

This convergence of the mountains with the sea is always absorbing and inspiring, but what the Dead Sea evokes is not tranquil harmony. The Dead Sea poses several physical and mental challenges to all who approach it. It's incredible to think that this impossible barrenness was such a fertile ground for human and cultural ferment from the early days of Jericho nine thousand years ago, through biblical Sodom, the Nabatian, Jewish, and Hellenistic settlements of the Second Temple period, to the tourist industrial projects of the last decades. This marvellous area, where everything is glaringly exposed and at the same time veiled and intriguing, instils you with a perplexing feeling, intermittently pleasant but somewhat troubling as well. If you come here enough times throughout the years, you too will accrue memories to weave into the big story.

When Sodom Arad Road ends, on the way to the coastal strip of Ein Bokek, where most of the hotels in the Dead Sea are, we pass the Dead Sea Works plant, which at night looks like a huge spaceship. For years, these immense machines have been evaporating water to produce potash in commercial quantities, and they are part of the reason it's disappearing at a horrifying rate. I'm trying to remember whether Shiri from PR also represents the owner of the plant while phoning her again, unsuccessfully. I quickly scan the lobby overlooking the pool. Herds of vacationers, tiredly sailing their flip-flops, producing the familiar Israeli noise of speech within an inch of yelling. I look at Tzachi–I already recognise the little tics that start to seize him when he goes for too long without smoking or drinking something, and to preempt future disagreeableness, I suggest we visit the bar at the edge of the lobby.

Only inside of it do I realise it's a traditional Irish bar. A heavy oak tree, stout barrels, clovers and green elves hanging from every corner, and plasma screens broadcasting highlights from a match between Bolton and Sunderland which took place under torrential rain very far from here. "Who the fuck builds an Irish pub in the Dead sea?" I ask Tzachi, who is already ordering "a pint of Guinness and a shot of Jameson" from the languid Palestinian bartender. Somehow his Irish accent is flawless. "You need to be more positive," he says dryly. I order a Guinness too, and after a few sips our spirits pick up and we begin to jovially chat up two middle-aged couples who came here as part of a weekend package for their workers' committee, which includes a show by a famous Mizrahi music singer and a lecture on love and kabbalah. The women are flattered by our attention and the men continue to stare at the screen apathetically. The rain in Sunderland is only getting stronger. The ball bounces blindly on the wet grass. After a few moments I'm starting to picture this quartet having sex and to sink into deep despair, when suddenly a young woman in a subtle T-shirt and tight jeans appears in the crowd. She is obviously not on vacation here and also obviously on her way to us.

"Shiri from Bar-de Haan-Yakin. I got your message. We can't give you an interview with Leonora. We promised exclusivity to the competing newspaper, and we don't see why the political reporter needs to interview the most famous actress in Latin America. We're actually a little apprehensive about it."

"I like Leonora—I thought we could give a slightly different angle on the whole story."

"Different how?"

"Maybe she can say a few words about the conflict?"

"We don't discuss our relationships with business associates or competitors, and the whole affair with the previous CEO... Wait, which conflict are you talking about?"

I feign a naïve look. Shiri sighs. "I'm sorry they sent you all the way here. I'm not interested in politics but Yakini says you're a good writer, and I know your crazy boss will insist that you get this story at any cost. But you'll have to leave now. You're not guests at the hotel and it's booked to capacity today. I checked with the manager."

Shiri leaves. Three security guards and a manager had been watching us from a distance. The women at the adjacent table smile, curious to see what we'll do next. The men continue to watch the game. The security guards take a few steps in our direction. Tzachi has somehow ordered another Guinness at some point and is finishing it with a long sip. We go outside.

In the car, Shimi the editor calls and says if we don't bring him at least a photo and one quote from Leonora–doesn't matter what–he's "cutting our guts open and feeding them to the cats at the Carmel Market". I have no idea why we're taking him seriously but we are, presently trying to imagine where they might be shooting with Leonora. We decide to proceed north towards Ein Gedi, where the hotel we'll be staying in is–thanks to a barter agreement made by the paper's marketing CEO, who suffers from psoriasis and tries to spend as much time in the Dead Sea as possible.

A bus of Korean tourists passes by us. They take photos of Mount Masada, which is on our left. Two thousand years ago, hundreds of Jews who were weary of the corruption and materialism in decadent Jerusalem came here to find a purer, more religious life. When the Roman armies besieged them, they preferred suicide to capitulation. This myth is still very much alive, and around the age of thirteen every Jewish Israeli comes here on a special school trip which includes staying the night in the nearby field school, receiving a wakeup call at 4am and climbing up the snake path–the original route used by the Jewish suicide rebels–to the top of the fortress, where a special ceremony is held before the students' parents. I remember something was troubling me that night and I couldn't fall asleep, and by the time we'd climbed up I was feeling so bad my mother had to take me down in the funicular while the other kids held the valour ceremony on the mountain. "Isn't it insane that they put kids through this?" I ask Tzachi, and realise he is asleep, the edge of his hair washing in the rays of sunlight hitting the windshield.

At the entrance to Ein Gedi beach I stop the car with a grinding screech. Tzachi wakes up annoyed. He picks up his camera case with great difficulty. We're greeted by a biting, unpleasant scent of sulphur. The entrance is crowded with tourists, mostly Russian, and with dozens of tables stocked with cosmetic and medicinal products. Tzachi comes to life, photographing the elderly Russian tourists, gradually focusing on one old woman who is eating a drumstick ice cream cone and looking a little ridiculous. When she looks up and notices Tzachi, she starts cursing him in Russian, but he just continues to take photos of her. Her bullish husband walks up to him and a confrontation is only averted thanks to the fortuitous intervention of a security guard. As the husband continues to curse him in Russian, Tzachi disappears into the wardrobes, going over the photos he'd taken as if all the fuss has nothing to do with him.

Since the coastline has moved so much farther away from where it was only a decade ago, a train harnessed to a tractor wagon takes the sweaty vacationers from the main area to the waterline. It's a few minutes' drive to the edge of the world. The rocks and waste scattered at the side of the road moan along with the vacationers under the heavy heat and barrenness. I see the reception on my phone is fading. On the shoreline are a few beds and thatches, young lifeguards and a few girls, probably from the neighbouring kibbutz, drinking vodka Red Bulls and laughing. Tzachi lights another joint and it's quickly digested in the dry hot air. It's hard to move here. We are carefully walking on the hot rocks, which quickly become a beautiful crystalline bed of salt, absorbed into the sea. The water is warm and oily and we cautiously get in. "Aaaahhh," Tzachi screams and I laugh. "This isn't a brothel," I tell him. "It burns," he keeps yelling, and everyone around is looking until he calms down. We lay on the water and start floating, slowly shedding the hardships of the day, the salt tingling the pores without hurting too much and then soothing us. The eyes wander from the skies to the wonderful mountains of Edom before shutting peacefully. Pleasant and abstract thoughts supplant their predecessors. Images from an old 8mm film I might or might not have seen flood my field of vision–three blonde women at the end of the Sixties, clutching an Uzi and laughing, swinging it at the camera. I think there was something I was supposed to do today.

I don't know how much time passes before I open my eyes again. I didn't notice the water carrying me so far from the beach. My eyes drift to a small cove in the northern shoreline. Something's twinkling there. At first I think it's a hallucination brought on by the drugs and the sun, but on a second look I see it's coming from a large piece of styrofoam surrounded by what looks like a camera crew, and in front of it–I'm now seeing–is a female model in a full-body bathing suit. I get myself together and try to stand in the water. I spray some water on my face and it burns my eyes. I start walking toward the beach but the water is heavy and I'm moving very slowly. I skip across the sharp gravel to wash myself in the showers. Around me are dozens of figures smeared in mud. I look for Tzachi but can't find him anywhere. His stuff is gone too. I grab my things and hurry towards the flickering light, moving on a hard space which, up until recently and for millions of years, has been covered in sea, and is now too exposed. I cross a makeshift fence at the end of the beach and then stop. The lack of minerals and water doesn't only bring about a vaporisation of the sea and move the bathing beaches farther and farther away from the shore, but also makes sinkholes–large depressions in the ground that suddenly gape and suck all they can into them–appear with increasing regularity. The sinkholes adumbrate new pathways, make footholds change their locations and roads change their routes. Nature avenges its vandals so parabolically and graphically, like an ecological horror picture written especially for this slab of earth. This hole is also what now denies me access to Leonora–a woman I'd only heard of yesterday, who has by now become the object of infinite desire. I must meet her, must get a picture of her, must get a quote out of her.

I hurry back to the jerry-built train that will take me to the road, and wait another fifteen minutes in the scalding heat for it to arrive. Eventually I'm back at the main vicinity but Tzachi is missing. Only after forty-five minutes of sweaty anticipation does he suddenly appear, peaceful and radiant, enthusiastically telling me about the massage he'd received from a proselyte German who fell in love with an Israeli New Age guru and moved into a cabbalist hippie community in Metzoke Dragot. I snatch the bag with the keys from him and run towards the vehicle, but running isn't really possible in this heat–everything is happening in a continuous slow motion. The Koreans' bus passes us again as we quickly come up on the main road, and I'm honking like an insane person–making a trail of German tourists panic and three camels resting at the side of a young Bedouin nuzz with disdain. We drive down a dirt road that quivers the chassis of the small Japanese vehicle and eventually reach a small anchorage. About two hours have passed from the moment I'd seen them until I got here, and the crew is already wrapping up and loading the rest of the equipment into a commercial vehicle. Leonora is making jokes with the makeup artist. I don't see Shiri or any security guards anywhere. I approach Leonora and introduce myself as a journalist from the competing publication who will be interviewing her.

"I thought we were meeting in the evening," she smiles obligingly. A thin white cloth covers her full bathing suit. Beads of water are still twinkling on her smooth skin. There is nothing in her body that isn't perfect.

"I wanted to see you at work."

"I've been up since 5am, but this landscape is wonderful. It's a great honor for me to shoot at such a beautiful and unique place, for such an original and innovative company."

"Is there a message you would like to send the Israeli public?"

"I want to tell them that their love moves me in a new way every time. That they're always on my mind and that even when I'm far my heart is with them. I have many fans in many places but only a small part of them are here, in the land where Jesus was born, and where so many miracles happened in the past. I look at my relationship with the Israeli fans as a big miracle also, made out of many little miracles, and I feel that God has sent me here."

Her smile is perfect. I look back at the car to make sure Tzachi's getting all this. Now my moment has come.

"How do you think the Palestinian people would respond to your doing advertising for an Israeli company with plants in an occupied territory?"

Leonora becomes silent. The idyllic veil has been rended. She looks around for help. Her face sobers. I've done this to so many interviewees in the past, but something about this woman's face makes my heart crumble.

"I don't think I'm supposed to answer that question." She's helplessly signalling the assistant, who arrives in a panic. She whispers something to her. The assistant looks at me angrily. "What did you say your name was?" She dials the iPhone with one hand and beckons two security guards with the other. I retreat backward, signalling Tzachi to move to the driver seat and start the car. To my surprise he does this with maximal efficiency. We take off without looking back.

Within a few minutes we're at our hotel in Kibbutz Ein Gedi. What started as a humble guesthouse is slowly expanding and becoming a kind of sophisticated and over-expensive boutique hotel. We spend two hours in the nice pool on the edge of a cliff with a view to the sea. At sunset we walk along a new promenade overlooking Nahal Arugot. Two ibexes skip between the rocks in the wadi below. I call Tzachi's attention to them but he ignores me. Something about him will remain inscrutable to me forever. The hotel dining room is packed and, as in the Irish bar, most of the workers are Arabs. The buffet is stocked with diverse courses but I have never had anything good to eat at the Dead Sea and tonight's not going to be any different. Something about this place always thwarts the indulgence of hedonism. The desire for beauty, pleasure, and the money that makes them attainable, always comes up against a more mysterious, primordial element. It's a part of the intensity of the place, for good or ill. I fill my plate with a kiddie schnitzel and French fries and eat too much.

In the evening, pleasant air replaces the sweltering heat. We smoke another joint and walk between the botanical garden and the rooms. The people who built this place toiled and sweated to start a new social utopia. Their grandchildren sell spa packages to tourists from around the world. Tzachi says it's a shame the world has changed so much and I say I don't really miss anything. This kibbutz is an oasis covered in exotic plants. We hear playing from one of the open yards–a group of twenty men and women in their sixties is sitting around a table and singing in Russian. We come near them, they don't speak a word of English, but as it turns out Tzachi can speak basic Russian with them–I have no idea why and how–and it's as if they'd been his friends forever. They all have a genial look in their eyes, like true believers do, and they tell us how much they love Israel and how happy they are that we came to sit with them. They pretend to have not lost the thread when I sentimentally hold forth on the importance of Jesus in the world history of class division. Later they dedicate us a song and begin singing "How good and how pleasant it is for brethren to dwell together in unity" in Russian. We hum along with them, they in Russian and us in Hebrew, without knowing if there's any overlap between the two versions, and I think I haven't sung this song in years. Tzachi is moved, and he gives each one of them a big hug, and then retires–leaving me stranded before their cryptic smiles.

When I come back to the room Tzachi is sleeping. I take his camera to look at Leonora's photos. He took about forty of them during our short talk. They're all too highly exposed, completely washed out. In some of them you can discern an arm or a piece of cloth, but the famous actress is impossible to make out. I put the camera down. There's no story without these pictures. I fall into a heavy slumber and after a few hours wake up with a start.

I go outside. The sun begins to rise from the mountains of Edom. The kibbutz is still sleeping, and the beach under me is starting to clear, rendering into view with the Jordan mountains and the blue-green sea like a freshly taken Polaroid picture. Not far from it, at the northern edge of the sea, is Jericho, the most ancient existing settlement in the world. I remember going there on trips as a kid in the early Eighties, before the first intifada, when Israelis would travel the Palestinian territories practically freely. I remember the abandoned green swimming pools of ancient

Arab villas, a Trappist monastery with a rock-cut winery that seized my imagination, and my mother bargaining with a local merchant over a large clay pot that I can't remember if she ended up buying or not. When I went back there at the end of the Nineties to do a story on the casino that for a brief spell was one of the most profitable gambling establishments in the world, thanks to thousands of Israeli addicts who lost their life savings to it, the Austrian security guards wouldn't allow me to get far enough from the casino and hotel area to see whether the places I remembered were real. I wonder what became of those slot machines that were abandoned after Arik Sharon visited the temple mount and ignited the second intifada, which left thousands of casualties and probably irremediable degrees of hatred in its wake. What happened to the poker and blackjack tables. What happened to the Russian prostitutes, the Palestinian dealers, the taxi driver from Jerusalem who sobbed by the roulette at five in the morning when he realised his life had just been ruined.

The mountains and the water continue to clear slowly. Leonora, Shimi, the editor and Tzachi, Shiri, they're all probably still asleep, hovering between the ciphers of yesterday and the oracles of tomorrow, waiting to tackle a new day of desires, successes and failures, as this lake–the vestige of a tectonic collision from twenty-five million years ago–where nothing ever happened, except for a fathomless wrestle of chemicals and minerals, wakes up to a new day.

ONCE IN ROYAL DAVID'S CITY
by Julia Handelman-Smith

My first Christmas away from home was in the Holy Land. A lifetime of Christmas Eves had passed in the same rural village in the English Midlands, and with minor tweaks over the years had followed the same traditional patterns: carol singing around the village fuelled by mulled wine, midnight mass, and drinks in the pub with our friends and neighbours.

The decision to do something different was for practical reasons, rather than religious or ideological. I was living in Tel Aviv, and work commitments made it difficult to travel home. Instead, my parents would come to visit me and we would travel with other members of the Church of England community in a specially organised diplomatic convoy to Bethlehem. I did not feel like a pilgrim, but there it was, on my doorstep.

I had visited Bethlehem a few times before. The fast-track section for diplomatic cars made it fairly straightforward to pass through the intimidating checkpoint process, and I had spent afternoons walking around its sleepy streets. Rather too sleepy, for the birthplace of Jesus Christ. I was always quite unnerved by the lack of visitors in this this iconic place: the political graffiti that far outweighed religious symbols, and the temptation to haggle up for the beautifully carved olive wood nativity sets that local craftsmen create far faster than they can sell. This was Bethlehem in 2007, when decades of conflict, continuing Israeli settlement and a twelve-metre Israeli partition had splintered its communities.

Traditionally a Christian town, internal displacement within the Holy Land and the emigration of its conflict-exhausted inhabitants has shifted the demographic to a Muslim majority. Many pilgrims can experience the Christian story with more peace of mind within the Old City of Jerusalem, where they are also able to purchase Bethlehem's Christian souvenirs, albeit at an amazing mark-up. There is a lot of argument about the Christian communities in the Holy Land. Statistics state that the percentage of Christians has remained relatively constant since Mandatory times; however, that belies a lot of emigration overseas, either as a result of the 1947 conflict, or later for economic and quality of life reasons. Both of the major protagonists in the continuing conflict–Israeli and Palestinian–have been accused of unequal treatment of Christians. Both sides accuse the other of racist abuse and harassment of the Christian community.

But on 24 December some fifteen thousand people flock to the city, a pilgrimage that is repeated a few weeks later for the Orthodox celebrations. Political leaders from both Israel and Palestine, as well as senior figures from around the world, take part in a televised midnight mass from the ancient Church of the Nativity led by the Roman Catholic bishop of Jerusalem. Access to this VIP event is almost impossible, but we were joining a group of Anglican worshippers for a much smaller celebration led by the Anglican Bishop of Jerusalem earlier in the evening.

The Anglican Community in the Holy Land is a minority amongst minorities. With Christians in the Holy Land already a tiny slice of the overall population, Anglicanism is a pinprick amongst the Catholic, Orthodox and other numerous factions of the Christian faith. Over the years, different branches of the Christian community have developed complex arrangements of sharing the major Christian sites of the Holy Land, but no Anglican chapel exists at either the Church of the Nativity in Bethlehem or in its sister Church of the Holy Sepulchre in Jerusalem. In one of the many, but nevertheless incongruous, streaks of pragmatism that exist within religious communities, the Greek Orthodox community had loaned us their chapel on the site–unneeded for their Christmas celebrations until two weeks later.

As we gathered at the English church on Nablus Road, instructions were given to stick to the car in front. Our convoy sped recklessly along the short road to Bethlehem, slowing to a crawl as we manoeuvred through the narrow and crowded streets. Israeli soldiers, mostly youngsters completing their obligatory military service, waved us through the checkpoints and handed us over to the Palestinian police.

Because Christmas Eve in Bethlehem is not peaceful. A solidarity concert taking place in Manger Square featured performances from all over the world, and an audience of thousands thronged the square. Supporters of Bethlehem, or Palestine, or the Holy Land–or simply local people with a rare opportunity to see live art in their own town crowded the streets. Our attempts to reach the Church of the Nativity touched on the biblical. Every attempt to enter the church involved a heated debate with a policeman. Whilst the dignitaries at the front of our convoy drove to the church door with no difficulty, we found it hard to convince the authorities that we were also invited. Our cars were turned back and we had to try several routes and parking places before returning to the church on foot, and still the local police didn't want us to access the church. They had no idea that the Anglican community had arranged a small celebration ahead of the official Catholic service at midnight.

I grew increasingly uneasy: it had been a mistake to put my parents through an experience that was rapidly turning into an ordeal. Whilst the police officials were very cheerful, they waved their large guns around in a very casual way and spoke animatedly and loudly. I realised how anaesthetised I had become to the military states of the Holy Land: armed checkpoints and teenage soldiers with heavy weaponry on the streets of Tel Aviv. My parents, quietly spoken people from a peaceful English village where regular policemen don't even carry a handgun, were finding the whole process pretty unnerving. Normally, the most confrontational part of Christmas might be the jostle at the pub bar, and by now they had seen more military hardware this evening than they had in their lives. Added to that, none of us spoke Arabic and we started to realise that should we be split up from our group, we would have no idea how to get home.

Eventually, miraculously, we found ourselves stooping through the tiny door of the church, built to deter mounted crusaders from entering on horseback. There were probably only about one hundred of us, but we filled the tiny space, standing or perched on stone steps and the odd chair. We were led through an informal, multilingual service of readings, prayers and carols with no hymn sheets or service books. Often we sang carols to a familiar tune, each person singing the well-worn words of their own language. Coming from a tradition where much of the celebration of Christmas is attached to the choreography of music, candlelight and ceremony, it could not have been further from a traditional

Christmas. Yet, perhaps because our journey to Bethlehem had been so fraught, the rather stilted version of "Silent Night" in several different languages had more meaning than it does on a quiet village green. Silence, after all, is much more appreciated if you have also experienced cacophony and chaos.

About halfway through the service there was a sudden rush of cameras as Palestinian Authority chairman Mahmoud Abbas arrived to address the congregation. He spoke for five or ten minutes and left, followed by his retinue of journalists and supporting staff. I remember little of what he said now, but he spoke of peace and the importance of Christmas in bringing communities and people together. But despite this, the moment jarred with the rest of the ceremony. This rare opportunity for people from many different communities to come together and celebrate privately was plunged back into the world of conflict and insecurity just outside the church walls.

Because Christmas in the Holy Land, like everything else, is political. Even an apolitical speech is a political statement. It is impossible to think about the holy city of Bethlehem without drawing attention to its plight and the daily uncertainty of its citizens.

We quickly recovered, and the service ended with a haunting solo of a traditional Palestinian carol. And it was in that moment that I realised that I had finally shaken off the stress and confusion of our short but highly-charged journey to Bethlehem. Although brief, it was a moment of complete serenity, because I could think of nowhere else I would rather be at that moment than here. Afterwards, we filed out of our tiny chapel and visited the grotto of the nativity, and enjoyed a brief but exceptional moment in the larger part of the church, emptied of tourists and worshippers in preparation for the politicians to arrive for the main event later in the evening. I had no envy or curiosity about attending what was obviously the main event in Bethlehem that evening–or even that year. I felt more privileged to have attended our improvised, quieter service.

We spent Christmas Day in Tel Aviv, celebrating quietly at home amongst a community that sees it as another ordinary day in the working calendar. Without our Bethlehem visit, I'm not sure we would have remembered it was Christmas ourselves. Most of my Christian friends in Israel celebrate the Orthodox Christmas (either Greek or Russian) in early January, and from the wall-to-wall sunshine to the traffic and bustle of a normal working day, there was nothing in our surroundings to remind us of Christmas.

Two Christmases later, my mother-in-law, Sari, joined us in Hickling, Nottinghamshire to experience her first ever Christmas. Although thousands of miles from the Holy Land, she enjoys something closer to the traditional Christmas she expects from thousands of western depictions: carol singing with mulled wine, midnight mass and the pub. She excitedly points to "Bethlehem" in all of our traditional carols, and we laugh because it is so close–no more than an hour away–from her home in Israel. But for Sari, Bethlehem is as distant and as iconic as it is to the other carollers, only for different reasons. Bethlehem is both a religious and a political icon in the Holy Land, and whilst for we middle-Englanders it is physically far and raised to mythical status by our religion and culture, for both of us it is made even more inaccessible because of conflict. In ordinary circumstances, there would not be many barriers to visiting Bethlehem these days. But ironically Bethlehem has maintained its mystery, shielded–or overshadowed–by a conflict that that has become almost as iconic as its religious significance.

I haven't spent Christmas in Bethlehem since, choosing to return to my traditional western roots. For my parents, too, once seemed to be enough. However, my experience of Bethlehem has entered the fabric of my Christmas. Although I would borrow the words of the late Johnny Cash and describe myself as a "C-minus" Christian, the Christmas of 2007 reminds me of so many things about the Christmas story and what it is supposed to mean to be a Christian. Albeit in modern times, I have a fragment of empathy for the trauma of a young pregnant woman, seeking refuge in Bethlehem amongst thousands of others. I can also associate this with the thousands of people today who continue to struggle to live in Bethlehem. But beyond that, I also remember a group of people stumbling their way through "O Little Town of Bethlehem" in whatever language they know, and a very rare, and equally brief, moment of private peace in the Holy Land.

THE JERUSALEM SYNDROME
by Julia Handelman-Smith

A lot is said, even between the covers of this book, about the invisible walls that divide the Holy Land. Most cities retain a distinct character: Jewish, Arabic Christian, Arabic Muslim, Druze. Yet despite lying at the heart of the Holy Land conflicts, Jerusalem's Old City maintains a brittle but functioning peace where Muslim, Jewish and Christian communities live cheek by jowl. Barely changing over several centuries, not least because the slightest alteration can cause mayhem not only between, but within communities, a walk through the Holy City captures both a sense of times past as well as (on a good day) what a peaceful Holy Land might look like.

If you can, and it is not too hot, start at the Mount of Olives. Here you will get the iconic view of the ancient city and the Golden Gate. This is the first shot taken for every documentary or newsreel, and it doesn't disappoint. Walk down the hill (taking the road) and stop halfway at the Garden of Gethsemane, which remains a peaceful spot often left off the pilgrimage trail for being slightly out of the city centre.

Continue towards the city and enter the Muslim Quarter of the Old City through St Stephen's, or the Lions' Gate. If you haven't already guessed, you are taking the route many believe Christ took on his journey to the crucifixion, the

Via Dolorosa. Although this has recently been contested by archaeological findings it is still a route of pilgrimage for Christians, with signs en route to show different stages of Christ's journey. However, you are still in the heart of a modern city, and on this part of the route there will even be groups of young men hanging out on a Saturday afternoon. Some shopkeepers may invite you to see the "real" stages of the cross, often one or two floors below street level because the ancient city of Jerusalem was said to be at least five metres below the present-day city. Single female travellers should beware–this may include an (un)welcome proposition at station five that requires a hasty exit!

At the junction, stop at the Austrian hospice on the right for a touch of old colonial charm. Elegant but worn, the café has a great sachertorte if you've already overdone it on the falafel and baklava. Most important is to get up onto the roof of the building for another fine view of the city, which you can probably enjoy in solitude.

From here, take a left and immediate right and enter the labyrinth of the ancient souk. Directions at this stage are useless–the best part is to get lost. If you're keen, you can continue to follow the stations of the cross, not least because this brings you into the Church of the Holy Sepulchre by the best route, which is through the Ethiopian and Coptic monasteries on the roof of the St Helena Chapel. At some point in the souk, you have passed the seamless divide into the Christian Quarter of the city, but a quick trip down HaNotsrim leads you past the Jaffa Gate entrance to the city and into the much quieter Armenian Quarter. This is where you will find some of the more peaceful monasteries and Christian guesthouses in the city; the Armenian Garden and Cathedral of St James are worth a stop.

Moving back eastwards, you finally enter the Jewish

Quarter of the city, and modernity slowly enters back into the Old City. Many Jewish communities have moved back to this part of the city since 1967, and it has become a prime area of real estate. Consequently, there is more renovation and visible affluence here than in other parts of the city. Finally, don't be put off by the security to enter the Western Wall plaza and to visit the Temple Mount.

By this stage you have just about done a full circle, and might be needing a break from religion, full stop. I'd recommend heading south-west to the Jerusalem Cinematheque or north to the American Colony Hotel: both offer tranquil, secular spots for quiet meditation.

MY LIFE AS A DOG IN EAST JERUSALEM, OR SMELLY WALKS
by Karin Gatt-Rutter

My name is Ramses and I am a boxer from Haifa. At the early age of six weeks I moved to my home in Sheikh Jarrah. Sheikh Jarrah is located north-east of the famous American Colony Hotel and houses many diplomatic missions, the Office of the Middle East Quartet, and two hospitals, St John's and St Joseph's. The latter I visited once, by mistake, as I managed to get off my leash and run after some kids. Everyone was screaming and I thought it was a lot of fun. But I was just five months old. Today, I would of course know that hospitals are off-limits for dogs.

I am lucky because my house is big and I can also roam around in the garden where I chase cats–but sometimes they scare me, although I am bigger; cats in East Jerusalem are not to be messed with, I have learned.

I go out on dog walks normally in the neighbourhood. I am still very undisciplined and therefore have to be on the leash. It is OK–you get used to it after a while.

Most of my walks are along Route 1, along the so-called Green Line which marks the division between Israel and the territories captured in the Six-Day War. It has nice green lawns on the side of the busy two-lane roads in each direction, and bushes and trees. But before reaching the green and smelly spots I have to pass the open-air sports ground, where even at six in the morning women and men, mostly from east Jerusalem, walk or run in sports gear or traditional clothing, and the Spanish consulate general facing the sports ground. I adore the funny hats that the Guardia Civil guys wear.

I love to sniff around the containers of trash everywhere. It is amazing how much litter there is in this part of town! The scary thing is that there is a lot of broken glass, which can cut my sensitive paws.

I rarely meet any dogs–not too many people own dogs that go out on walks. But I can smell that there are other dogs around. I know there are wild dogs around the area close to the Ambassador Hotel or down in the valley from the Mount of Olives Road to Wadi Joz (the Walnut Valley). When I was a puppy they scared me with their barking and my mistress had to throw stones at them to make them run away. It is tough for dogs in this part of town. So, stone-throwing is good.

Another smelly walk is the area next to Route 1, heading north and passing the police headquarters. There, I hear and smell my canine brothers and sisters who are running around inside the fence. They never come close to the fence as I don't think they have a long leash. Before I head up to the statute I have to pass a dangerous road with many lights. I have to sit pretty and wait until it is green (not that I see the difference between green and red, but that is what my mistress tells me) before I can run up the hill. In the summer people sometimes have picnics there. They are mostly students from the Hebrew University who leave packages of fries or other things I can gobble up. But I know I am not allowed to eat from the ground. But who cares? I am a dog!

My bestest walk, though, is the Tabachnik Park, which is

part of the Mount Scopus Campus of the Hebrew University. There, if I am lucky, I get to run off the leash, as there are not too many people or dogs there. It has nice Mediterranean vegetation including trees to climb in, if I could. It has a magnificent view over the Old City of Jerusalem. In fact many people come in buses to stop and look at the view and take photos. But they never come into the park.

When it is too hot my mistress brings a special water bottle, which is a gadget I can drink from the way we dogs drink. Once I could also lick water from the sprinkler system of the Jerusalem municipality. The plastic tubes had dog-convenient holes.

As I said, I love the rubbish containers with everything in them that humans throw away. It would be great to have a treasure hunt one day. I know I would do very well because once I found a black bra.

Ramses

PART THREE: TZAFONA

(In ancient Hebrew, the north was called Tzafona or Semola, meaning "left", which is like the Arabic Shamal, as in north.)

IN THE NAME OF THE FATHER
by Shay Fogelman

My father was one of the conquerors of the Golan Heights.

On the noon of 9 June 1967, he and the Eighth Armoured Brigade stormed the black basalt mountains with cannon fire. They led the battlefront and encountered fierce Syrian resistance. Most of the tanks of the first battalion were hit in the first hours of fighting. Many soldiers were killed or wounded, but six more Israeli brigades joined the attack later that day. The war ended the next day.

During the six days of the war, my father and the Israel Defense Forces (IDF) fighters defeated the armies of ten Arab countries. The accumulated territory they occupied was three times larger than Israel had been before the war.

Six years later, in October 1973, my father fought in the Golan Heights once again. Like hundreds of thousands of other Israelis, he was called in the middle of Yom Kippur, the most sacred day for the Jewish people, to go defend the land from the Egyptian and Syrian armies, which had launched a surprise attack from their respective fronts. This time, my father was added to the Seventh Armoured Brigade as a reservist. The brigade's confrontation with Syrian forces in the northern Golan is considered one of the most heroic battles of the war to this day. For four days of battle, my father and the brigade soldiers barely succeeded in holding back an armoured Syrian force that outnumbered them six soldiers to one. Half their tanks were hit. Many of them were killed.

I was born between the two wars, between the euphoria of the 1967 victory and the collective mourning that enfolded the country after the Yom Kippur War. In one of his poems, the wonderful Hebrew poet, Shaul Tchernichovsky, wrote, "Man is nothing but the image of his native landscape." My native landscape is a country in conflict, blood pouring from its borders, the names of conquerors and wars outlining its history books. Although I grew up in one of Tel Aviv's grey suburbs in the middle of Israel, the Golan Heights played an important role in shaping my conflicted childhood landscape.

When I was a child, my father would take my little brother and me on trips to the Golan almost every summer. Sometime we would spend a few nights in a tent or under the sky, by the fire. I loved the trips in the Golan Heights; the wonderful landscapes, the wildlife, all the historical sites. My father always brought along topographic maps, history books, and plant and bird guides. He taught me how to navigate the turf by myself, how to identify poisonous summer snakes, and how to purify the stream waters before I drank them. At night he taught me how to light a fire with a single match, how to brew excellent tea from leaves we'd picked up in the area, and how to find the north with the stars in the sky as my only guide. I loved the trips to the Golan Heights, especially spending time with my father, who knows every stream and path in the Golan very well.

The Golan Heights are in northern Israel, next to the border with Lebanon, Jordan and Syria. It is a tall, flat region. In its east rise several volcanoes shaped like trimmed cones. The Golan soil is hard. The rocks are black. The streams are steep and narrow. It is a tough and battle-scarred land.

The Israelites fought for it in the Bible. One of the decisive battles of the Great Revolt was waged in the Golan during the Roman period. In the seventh century AD it was the scene of the Battle of Yarmouk, which led to the fall of the Byzantine Empire and the Muslim conquest of the land. The memory of that battle remains one of the preeminent symbols of world jihad.

Human settlement in the Golan was among the most ancient in the world, and there are several spectacular archaeological sites in the area, some dating back to prehistoric times. In the eastern Golan Heights there's the "Wheel of Ghosts" (Rujm el-Hiri), a mysterious monument of stone circles surrounding a fifteen-foot-tall tumulus. The most outlying circle is 520 feet wide and archaeologists estimate that the site was constructed six thousand years ago, long before Stonehenge.

My father and I visited many archaeological sites in our summer trips to the Golan. I mainly remember the visit to the excavations at the city of Gamla, which was destroyed during the Jews' rebellion against the Romans in 67 AD. The city was built as a fortress, surrounded from three directions by a tall and steep cliff. It took the Romans two attempts to subdue the Jewish rebels. Four thousand Jews died in the fights. Another five thousand refused to surrender and jumped to their deaths from the cliff. I read all this as a child, in the book *The Wars of the Jews* by the historian Flavius Josephus. I received it after visiting the site as a gift from my father.

We also walked in the wild nature a great deal. The wars have left desolation almost everywhere, and you find remnants of bunkers, entrenchments, fences and minefields wherever you turn. In many places, human entry has remained forbidden and the vegetation has grown wild. The small civilian population in the Golan allows Mediterranean nature to grow practically freely in a large part of the territory. The last bears and tigers were hunted a hundred years ago, but foxes, wolves, hyenas, wild boar and a great variety of other animals are still around.

I remember a hike we took in Nahal Yehudia, a trail in the southern Golan that includes a thirty-foot-high waterfall. You can go around it through a narrow path, but you can also jump into the little water pool that was formed under it. It's a very dangerous leap because of the rocks hiding in the water. I won't forget the first time I stood at the head of the waterfall and looked down into the placid water. I repeated my father's instructions to myself. "Jump far. Watch for the rock on the right. Dive with both legs. When you come back up, stay clear of the thorny bushes." I was very afraid. I was more afraid of being a coward. I jumped.

The wars also played a part in our Golan trips. On the drive, my father would show us the Israeli lines of defence, the fortifications and the attack paths of the Syrian tanks. For dozens of years the two sides entrenched themselves and created one of the most complex aggregates of trenches, embankments, minefields and other barriers for storming forces in the world. Sometimes we would stop on an isolated hilltop and look over the border to the ruins of the town of Quneitra, which was ravaged in the battles and has remained empty and deserted. Then my father would tell us about the war. He would describe the battles and point to the places where his friends were killed. Once he told us about a Syrian plane that dropped bombs on an armed convoy of theirs, killing some of his friends. He remembered their names well and described the joy of life that was interrupted. He talked about sleepless nights, shooting and bombing sounds, the smell of gunpowder. He described the sights from the

Ruins of a Syrian village

Syrian military camp

morning after the battle: burnt tanks, bullet-marked jeeps, the corpses of soldiers, Syrian and Israeli.

Ever since its occupation in the '67 war, the Golan has been the main bone of contention between Israel and Syria. The border is usually quiet. Quieter than Israel's other borders. But tension and wariness around it persist. The Syrian claim towards Israel is simple: "You took it, give it back." Israel argues that there was no other choice. In several skirmishes that took place before the war, Syrian cannons fired at agricultural settlements by the border. Throughout the years, a number of Palestinian organisations have sent armed squads through the border to carry out actions against civilian population in Israel. When questions about the future of the Golan come up, many Israelis ask who is to guarantee that such things won't happen again if the Golan is returned. This is what my father fears as well. "The death toll we have paid for this land is too high," he tells me every time I bring up the possibility that a peace agreement leads to the cession of the Golan. I'm concerned about the blood that is yet to be spilled.

Israel has other excuses for retaining the Golan Heights. A considerable number of the water sources of the Kinneret, the largest freshwater lake in the country, are in the Golan. Mount Hermon, the highest mountain in Israel, is also in the Golan, and there are military intelligence facilities of great importance on its summit. The Israeli security establishment defines it as a strategically significant site. Although few would admit it, many Israelis will also have a hard time giving up Mount Hermon because its top is the only place where it snows in the winter, making it the only skiing site in the country.

Another issue that complicates a future peace agreement between the two sides concerns the Jewish settlement in the

Golan. Since its occupation, thirty settlements have been founded in the Golan, and today, about twenty thousand Israeli citizens live there, along with twenty thousand Syrian citizens, mostly from the Druze community, who remained in their five ancient villages at the foot of Mount Hermon after the Israeli occupation. There's another Syrian village under Israeli sovereignty between the Golan and Lebanon called Ghajar, whose inhabitants are Alawites.

As a child, I paid many visits to the Druze villages in the Golan Heights. Almost every time my father and I came, we would stop to eat at one of the local restaurants and finish with a cup of coffee. Most of the Druze community lives in the Middle East. The Druze practice a secret religion which was developed from Shia Islam and they believe in reincarnation, among other things. They are known around the Middle East for being valiant fighters. They have managed to survive as a small minority for hundreds of years, mainly thanks to their loyalty to every sovereign and opposition to every conqueror. They are mountaineers, obstinate folk living in a very conservative and traditional society.

My summer trips to the Golan Heights with my father stopped when I reached adolescence. I preferred going to the desert or to other areas of the country with friends my own age. My father was disappointed. He kept going back up to the Golan but said it wasn't the same anymore without my little brother and I. But what pained him most in that period was how, as my political stances began to crystallise, I became firmly opposed to the Israeli occupation of the Golan Heights and to visiting the region.

The change was gradual. For many months I read every book, article and opinion piece I could find about the Arab-Israeli conflict. I audited lectures, met with peace

Israeli tank positioned on the Syrian border

activists, even started learning a little Arabic, and came to acknowledge my people's collective responsibility for the conflict's history and for its future. At first my father regarded these stances as part of my teenage rebellion. Later he even forbade me from going to meetings with Palestinian activists and Israeli leftists who resisted the ongoing occupation of the West Bank and the Golan. Of course, I kept going behind his back.

My political dispute with my father wasn't resolved over the years. He's still convinced that the state of Israel must keep control of the occupied Golan and even planned to move there a few years ago. Thankfully, my mother was adamantly opposed to the idea. I could easily attribute the source of our differences to his war experiences or to the generational gap between us, but things are more complicated. My father sees the Golan Heights as a homeland where Jewish history has been developing for thousands of years. The ruins of the Jewish city of Gamla, which was destroyed in the Roman period, the vestiges of the Katzrin synagogue which was built in the Byzantine period, and even the Jewish settlement in the Golan at the end of the nineteenth century, which began long before the founding of the state of Israel, all reinforce the connection he feels to the place. I prefer to look at the future, and am positive that we must leave the Golan Heights and reach a peace agreement with Syria, even tomorrow morning if possible.

However, in recent years I've returned to the Golan Heights many times. I had a deep journalistic interest in the tradition of the Druze villagers and in their complex identity as a minority living under an occupation. My meetings with them produced a number of articles I published in *Haaretz*. One article concerned the Druze who served as

Syrian soldiers in the war of 1967. I was curious to know what fighting against my father was like and what the Israeli occupation looked like through their gunsights.

Many of the fighters I tracked down wouldn't speak to me. They don't give interviews to Israeli journalists, who they still consider their enemies. Others were very apprehensive and agreed to talk about the events of the war but refrained from describing their parts in it. I was surprised to discover that after so many years, many of them still feel humiliated by the defeat. Naturally, I kept my father's part in that war to myself.

Another article investigated a Druze spy ring that operated before the Yom Kippur War. I found that its members passed crucial information to Syrian intelligence, which brought Syria great success in the first days of the war. None of them has expressed any remorse, even though some have spent decades in Israeli prison. On the contrary, they are proud of what they did for their homeland to this day. I didn't tell them about my father and his friends who died in action either.

One of the investigations that yielded the most discoveries came about unexpectedly, when I heard from a Druze villager that until the war, tens of thousands of Syrians resided in a number of towns and villages in the Golan. This surprised me. In the Israeli history books and in my research on the wars in the region I never read about what became of the Syrian villages, towns and farms. My father didn't mention a civilian population when he described the wars in the Golan, and I never saw any traces of civilian settlements on our trips, only dozens of bunkers and army camps.

For several months, I rummaged through the archives and interviewed Israeli combatants and officers and Druze still living in the Golan, uncovering secret military documents

The cadet school of the Syrian army, now abandoned

and new testimony. I found that a substantial part of the Syrian civilians living in the Golan had left their homes right after the war broke out. Most of them had left because they feared the battles, and later the IDF prevented them from returning to their homes. But I also discovered that there were instances of organised evacuation, in which the few residents who remained in the villages were put on army trucks and transferred over the border with the aid of the International Red Cross. Their homes were either bulldozed or blown up in the months after the war. Israel only left the army camps in their place, serving a widespread myth about the Fearful Golan Heights.

Unlike the other territories Israel occupied in 1967, which either remained under military administration or belong to the Palestinian Authority, the Golan Heights were nationalised in the early Eighties. By means of a controversial law, a way for prime minister Menachem Begin to compensate the parties of the right for his agreeing to return the Sinai peninsula to Egypt in the Camp David accords, the government decided to apply Israeli law to the Golan. No country in the world acknowledges this annexation and the UN Security Council has unanimously adopted a resolution calling on Israel to annul it. The Druze residents of the Golan started a popular struggle against it and went on strikes that were quickly repressed by the authorities. The law has allowed them to become Israeli citizens, but few of them have. Most of them still view themselves as Syrian patriots living under an occupation. They have special resident IDs, don't vote in the Israeli elections, and are exempt from military service. They are entitled to education, medical care and other civil services in both countries. No one in Israel but them gets permission to cross the border to visit relatives in a country defined as an enemy state.

The Syrian civil war in recent years has further complicated the issue of the Golan Druze's identity. Some of them support the dictatorial rule of the Assad family, while others identify with the rebel forces. The side they choose could prove to be crucial for some of them. The Druze are a small minority in Syria, and several mass slaughters have already been carried out against them by each of the warring sides.

The Syrian civil war also keeps a political agreement with Israel and a solution to the question of the future of the Golan from being reached. The government in Syria is busy surviving. It has neither the motivation nor the ability to come to a peace agreement with Israel right now. No element in the opposition forces is capable of reaching any such agreement either, and ironically, this perplexing state of affairs allows my father to keep travelling in his beloved Golan, for the time being.

Grandpa Hillel

GALILEE MYTH
by Nili Landesman

I recently found myself seated on a bus, ready to embark on a four-hour pilgrimage to Tel Chai. Though the two words, "tel" and "chai" mean "mount' and "life" respectively, I have always referred to Tel Chai as the yard of blood–a reconstructed place of worship and myth, for those who see no choice but to live by the sword.

Each year a memorial service is held in Tel Chai to commemorate the eight men and women who died in combat on 1 March 1920–the story goes that the rest of the defenders withdrew from the battleground, leaving it to be burnt to the ground by the Arab attackers.

Seated at my bedside, my late grandfather, Hillel Landesman, would tell me the story of the immortal hero, Joseph Trumpeldor, commander of the isolated bloc in the upper Galilee Valley. My grandfather was one of the few to survive the battle that fateful day. He passed away in 1973, having never missed the annual memorial service held at the old cemetery, a few kilometres away from the famous courtyard, beneath the giant paws of the Lion of Judah perched atop the grave.

My grandfather was actually in the room when Trumpeldor gave up the ghost. Thirty-five years later, as chairman of the Galilee regional council, he gave a speech in which he stated "a miracle did not happen to us, although it was Purim". He went on to remind those present of the words written by the great Labour leader, Berl Katznelson, in response to an article written by his political opponent, Ze'ev Jabotinski (who had expressed his doubts regarding the necessity of this semi-suicidal act): "The only proof for our right upon our land is in this stubborn and desperate withstanding, without looking back."

That morning was indeed beautiful. Sunshine and raincloud battled overhead, and as I rode the bus I reread the protocol created for the conference held a week before the fall of Tel Chai. In a room full of giant Zionist key figures (such as David Ben-Gurion and Yitzhak Tabenkin), Jabotinski was the only person brave enough to suggest that it would be more responsible to evacuate the defenders. As the politicians argued, the defenders (as they used to call them back then) felt abandoned. Well, you can't argue with the Zionist karma, can you?

That day the guest of honour was the deputy minister of defence, Danny Danon, who had served as head of the Betar movement founded by Jabotinski. The founder had adopted Trumpeldor as the movement's iconic hero. Danon gave the main speech at the cemetery in front of hundreds of kids, members of the youth group, armed with whistles and decorated for Purim. Jabo's name popped up frequently. Did Danon even remember that Jabo's guiding spirit was actually against the whole mess? "We still have so many Trumpeldors," Danon declared loudly, "the settlers of Yehuda and Shomron."

The valley spread out at our feet, and I tried to visualise it under a thick blanket of snow, the way it was back in 1920, quiet, legendary, frightful. A little girl approached the bench where I was seated with my nineteen-year-old son Emanuel. "Is this a cemetery?" she wondered, "Is this a grave?"

When I was her age and lived in the kibbutz that gave shelter to fugitives from Tel Chai, I spent many happy hours in this graveyard. All those mysterious dead relatives made it feel great to be a daughter of the tribe.

Yitzhak, my eighty-four-year-old father, picked us up. The parking lot was packed with rented buses. "Once upon a time," Papa said as we hit the road, "back then in the early Fifties when we were still on top, Ben-Gurion needed to break the resistance for the reparations agreement between Israel and Germany. So he filled twenty-six buses with young, strong *kibbutzniks* from across the land, armed with clubs. Dad was there with them, enjoying a rare trip to Tel Aviv, the big city, on their way to beat the shit out of the other side—those guys from Betar, asking for trouble, protesting against the agreement in the main square. I was on those buses as a teenager, whenever the peace movement needed mass."

So hard, so sad, that you have to pick a side, especially if you live in a tradition of telling yourself a lie in the name of "truth". The spectacular kibbutz of my youth, Ayelet Hashachar, located a half-hour drive from Tel Chai, is named after the morning star. The story of how fifteen pioneers came up with this poetic name had been told to us many, many times before the lights were turned out. We would be sent to our beds with vivid impressions of that final scene—the hardworking dreamers, after spending the entire night arguing, suggesting and rejecting names, suddenly heard their colleague, the night guard, calling out, "Good morning, friends, the morning star is on the rise, time to get up and work." And they jumped and cried with joy, "We have found a name for ourselves!"

My dad was not one of the favourites when it came to putting us kids to bed. When he was on duty, no one joined us for our evening ceremony. He had no patience for those children's books–they were too long. So he would read one page to us, fast, skipping the next two pages. "They got stuck together," he would say, but I didn't mind. I could read them myself. It was easier to let him go. Yes, he was familiar with that romantic version of the story, but if he were to tell us the true story, how disappointed we would have been. *You want to know the truth? It just happened to be the Arab name of the place–Nijmat el Subach.*

It had been so long since I had visited this place, and I took a walk as the sun was setting. Ninety-nine years ago they came here, to the top of this hill, five men and one woman. This hill formed part of the land which–perhaps, perhaps not–once belonged to a small, perhaps large, village, Nijmat el Subach (that's how Dad pronounces it), that was located north-east from here, perhaps an hour's walk or more. Nijmat or "Njmat" (as it called on the Nakba map, which is considered to be a reliable Palestinian source) means "star". "El" means "of the", and so you can easily guess that "Subach" means "morning".

It was getting dark and chilly as I stood staring at the white square houses of the kibbutz. In 1923, they had moved from this original spot to the hill across the way, as the area had become too small. There were no good memories from this place. Life had been unbearable for the six pioneers, and they had had to leave by the end of their first year. Three of them returned, two years later, with more people and supplies. The original structure where I now stood, which exists only in photographs, had served as a house to the settlers and their animals. Now nature had taken over; above me a dark, clouded sky, over a hidden valley and rising mountain. Fields of young wheat stood silently. I could hear the birds in the trees, the frogs in the *vaddi* (the Arab word

*The Nijmat Settlers

Young Papa

for "stream") unloading all their secrets, the wind whispered beneath the sound of my footsteps. When I heard the jackals argue I became a little frightened.

There were no jackals here when I was a part of this broken dream. I had never been afraid to walk alone at night, nor sleep without my parents who were asleep in their own house. You were never alone, whether you were asleep or awake. We ate, played and had showers together, twenty kids well-trained to get along no matter what. When night finally came, you could always wait with anticipation for the moment when all the adults retreated to their lives, leaving us to be wild and crazy.

I couldn't remember the details; my memory was full of darkness. You don't need to remember that, I reminded myself, just focus on the past. There were no trees at all when young grandpa Hillel arrived here, at what is known as the "old Ayelet", on his way to join the defenders under siege in Tel Chai. This was the only resting point in a valley surrounded by Arabs, Bedouins and other tribes. All considered hostile, in our minds nothing more than names—Krad Bagara and Krad Ra'name, Achsaniya.

They had all fled by 1948. We tore these villages apart. Their names, however, were left with us to claim as we liked. Kibbutz Ayelet Hashachar is where the apples, pears and palm groves grow, where the cotton and cornfields can be found. If you spoke the dialect you would know where you were with the help of these Arab names. For us they were no more than waypoints for direction.

The following day, I spotted the morning star just above Krad Ra'name. I arrived at the kibbutz graveyard, so peaceful and beautiful, and as always, so well-kept. A silent place where you could talk as much as you liked. And besides, grandpa Hillel was half deaf. When he fought alongside Trumpeldor and his band of men, grandpa had lost his hearing. Unfortunately, it happened during the crucial fight and this is the story of how he had failed to hold his fire, when the replacing commander had shouted an order to do so.

Grandpa Hillel—every child in the kibbutz called him by this name, but he was most definitely my grandpa—didn't like to fight at all. According to the documents pertaining to the battle, he screwed up. That was his official job whenever things went wrong with the neighbours from differing tribes. Until his last day he held on to his utopia—that we should all learn to live together. If children could handle this, why couldn't the Jews and Arabs? Dad says his father was naïve, no big hero. He never fails to mention that his father didn't live to see the *kibbutzim* fall from grace. Clearly my dad has had it with this subject. The terrible stories he is rolling around in a glass of whisky—the once upon a time in the kibbutz—are not the kind you wish to tell a child

WE ALL GOT LOST IN THE SAME ANCIENT ALLEYS (VISITING KFAR KAMA)

by Nadia T Boshnak (Translated by Eilam Wolman)

If you ask me what makes a thing authentic and unique, I'll tell you–it's the packaging. Uniqueness grows in proportion to how small, humble and personal a thing is.

I'll explain. Picture a corner bookshop, not terribly large, with a plain, unadorned sign. The letter "K" is hardly noticeable anymore–it reads "Boo Store" and no one cares. The humble display window isn't lit at night, but if you pass by it in the day, you'll notice that it changes every few days. On one day, you would find novels there, at some other time autobiographies, on another day it would be children's stories that take you back to your own childhood. It has limited editions and rare books with autographs and personal dedications. If you try to search for it in the last pages of the weekend paper, where all the ads appear, you probably won't find it. It's reserved only for people who know it. The smaller and more personal it is, the more unique it is.

The store you've imagined with me exists somewhere very near you, and the reason you don't know it is because somebody else, probably your neighbour, would like it to remain his "secret bookshop", or his "secret pizzeria", or some other kind of secret.

My village, Kfar Kama, is small and authentic, like the

country it's in, like that secret shop in the corner. The country is so complex, the way its troubles come in bundles can be exhausting, but luckily, every evening I return to my village, my home, I understand that as troubled as it is, my country is worth it all. It's a magical place, and many before me have tried to capture that magic in words. But what makes my village special?

It's hard to say exactly. It may be how much all the residents, myself included, share in common, as if we were all raised by the same mother. How unified and pleasant the village is. We're all Circassians—Circassian is our mother tongue, although most of us also learned Hebrew, Arabic and English at a very young age. We're all Muslim; we were all brought up on the same traditional food, the same customs. We all got lost in the same ancient alleys as kids and all swept the street where we grew up at least once, because a great emphasis was always placed on cleanliness in the village. We even all had the same kindergarten teachers, and they are still a part of our lives, and we were all raised on the traditional story of our arrival in the land of Israel:

Our homeland lies near the north Caucasus Mountains, between streams and green fields. After it was conquered by the Russian empire, some of us were exiled to Europe and to the lands of the Mediterranean.

The journey was long and tough, and many didn't survive. At first, we moved to neighbouring Turkey. Although Turkey was Muslim, some of us were transferred to the Balkan countries under its rule designed primarily to defend the borders of the Ottoman Empire. We stayed in the Balkan area for fourteen years until the great uprising began, when some of the Bosnians and Circassians were transferred to Mediterranean countries.

Some of us had come from towns in the Kosovo area,

others came from Greece–together we were fifty thousand Circassians who sailed to the Middle East. The sea blustered and a fire started on one of the ships, leaving only seven hundred of the passengers alive. Only when they stood on dry land at the port at Acre in the north of Israel were they willing to believe they had survived. They were Shapsugs, one of the large tribes among the twelve Circassian tribes.

It was the spring of 1878 when we arrived in the land of Israel. A procession of wooden carriages drawn by bulls and horses slowly made its way from the Acre port, quietly crossing the coastal plain and turning east to Jezreel Valley.

The road was scattered with small villages and Bedouin encampments. Everything was new and strange to the immigrants: the inhabitants spoke Arabic, wore kafias and colourful clothes. Further east, overlooking the entire area, stood Mount Tabor, tall and round. The coaches went around the mountain and to the north-east.

Not long afterwards, the man in charge of the procession, who was the Turkish ruler, stopped.

"Ladies and gentleman," he turned to the people in the coaches.

"Here is where you'll be staying for now. Take down your things and sit here, until your permanent residence is determined." The immigrants looked around. The place was barren, desolate, derelict and ruined. Remnants of houses, shrub thickets, miserable-looking cabins.

"How could we settle here?" they asked.

"The place is entirely deserted and ruined; even the animals won't be able to survive here... and in our home country, along the River Afips, there was fresh greenery! It was a beautiful place! A Garden of Eden! How can we move from our paradise to this parched and desolate river?"

After some quiet, desperate moments, they looked at the

mountain they had passed. They saw the buds of flowers about to bloom, the emerging green in the fields and the caressing sun above them, portending the oncoming spring.

Without wasting much time, they began to build their home with inspiring mutuality, one house after the other. They put bars in all the windows and erected a tall wall to keep bandits and strangers from penetrating the yards, while retaining the beauty of the black basalt constructions, turning each of the yards, down to the smallest one, into a blooming orchard with a variety of fruit trees and flowers.

Before the streets in Kfar Kama were paved, the denizens would sweep the streets around their houses. Their perception to this day is that a house and the street it is in are inseparable. Organisation and cleanliness are a way of life, and every day you can see many of the village residents taking the time to clean up the streets.

One hundred and forty years have passed since those men, women and children built this little village I live in, along with 3,200 other residents. The children are still being raised on the same values and customs that our forefathers brought from the Caucasus. It seems like nothing has changed since then, apart from the buildings that now have a more modern style. However, the closer you get to the heart of the village, the alleyways get narrower and the architecture slowly changes. Blocks become basalt stones and live wires replace the high, hard walls. A picturesque scene emerges. You don't need to have grown up there to feel the historic atmosphere and to hear the past echoing in the sounds of the children playing, building their own childhood in that old place at that very moment.

In one of the alleys, you will find the fascinating Circassian Museum, run by Zoher Thawcho, where, among other things, you can see a performance of Circassian folk dancing.

The village includes many cafés and restaurants where you can taste Circassian delicacies such as pastries, kreplachs, and smoked cheeses.

There is another Circassian village in Israel called Rehaniya, which is in the Upper Galilee (Kfar Kama is located in the Lower Galilee, between the Sea of Galilee and Mount Tabor). The two villages have very close relations. Hundreds of thousands of Circassians are scattered elsewhere around the globe: Turkey, Syria, the United States, Germany, Jordan, and of course, the Caucasus.

HIPPIES
by Ithamar Handelman-Smith
(Translated by Julia Handelman-Smith)

The hippies are sitting on a bench next to a long, rough-hewn wooden table, the kind you see in Israeli nature reserves. We're sitting in the 1921 pub of Kibbutz Ein Harod Meuhad. The man has a red tilaka between his eyes. His hair is black, long, wavy. Pointy beard. His body long and slender. He is wearing a black knitted top, a short dark leather jacket, a wide black belt, purple gabardine flares, cowboy boots. On his chest, a gigantic silver medallion. The woman, a narrow, brown leather ribbon tied around her broad forehead. Wearing a pinkish sarong. Her hair bright, her eyes bright, her skin transparent–you could see her soul through it. Sahar, my friend, says that all people are transparent and you can see through them.

Sahar is a clever bloke. The way I see it, his wisdom is his obstacle. His abilities of observation and phrasing things, the way he sees and understands the world surrounding him–all of it brings a death wish upon him. One day, I say to him, your wisdom will kill you.

Sahar is fascinated by the medallion on the hippy's chest. The Freemasons, Sahar says, and I don't understand what he's talking about. This is the symbol of the Freemasons. The square and the compasses. I must talk to that hippy, he says, and approaches their table.

We don't speak the same language, but I can understand Sahar. I am urban, lower middle class, the offspring of Holocaust survivors. Something in Sahar's manner of speech testifies to his ancestry, his culture, his roots. He is the son of a kibbutz, an indigenous Israeli. His mum's family stretches back seven generations in the land of Israel. On his father's side, he is the grandson of one of the greatest mythological generals and members of Parliament of the Zionist movement. All the men in his family are high-ranking officers in top combat units. Sahar didn't serve in the army. He never wanted to take part in that story. But his Hebrew gives him away. I was afraid the hippies wouldn't understand him, thinking he was patronising or arrogant, but they said they're going with his flow, man. My brother, said the hippy that introduced himself as Hillel, doesn't have a clue what this medallion stands for. I just love it, man.

The girl, Renana, invited us for a round of Goldstar beer. Fast enough, it became clear that Sahar, Hillel and Renana have a mutual friend, Elifelet, from Beit She'an. Let's go all together to see Elifelet now, Sahar says, he's got something to smoke.

Sahar takes one of the communal kibbutz cars, a white Subaru, and we are driving to Elifelet's. It is the only time in my entire life that I have visited somebody in Beit She'an.

Elifelet looks a lot like Hillel, but he is bigger and broader than him. His hair long, curly, reaching the middle of his back. He is wearing a white Arabic tunic. He's got a didgeridoo in his house, djembe drums, a lute, stuff like that. Indian sitar music is playing in the background. We smoke Lebanese hash at his place, and we listen to different talk of "spirituality".

2.30am, Sahar wants to head back to the kibbutz, and he's offering Hillel and Renana a lift. They need to get to

Heftziba. Instead of going on Route 71, we're coming down Route 90, heading south towards Kibbutz Ein HaNetziv, and then we turn right on to Route 669. In the night-time the lorries that pass us look like prehistoric cattle. On our right, the man-made fish pools and on our left, the fig and eucalyptus groves. The car stereo is playing a CD of Creedence Clearwater Revival.

So where do you guys live, anyway, in Heftziba? Sahar is asking Hillel, who sits with Renana in the back seat.

No, only for the time being, until the house we're building will be ready, Hillel says.

And where is that?

Rotem, do you know it? Hillel says.

The road is empty, and Sahar slams the brakes.

What happened? I say. Is everything alright?

Rotem? Sahar repeats, and says, What is that? Where is that? It's in the Jordan Rift Valley, innit? It's beyond the Green Line. It's in the bloody Occupied Territories. It's a settlement, an illegal settlement.

Yes, my brother, but it's an ecological settlement, you know. No ideology or anything. What do I care about politics? I'm all in for peace, man, Hillel says, in a soft, gentle voice, as if there is no subtext, no underlying meaning to the fact that he is building a house in an Israeli settlement.

You are scum, you and your kind, Sahar says. Because of people like you, the worst things in history happened, and you are so stupid and dumb that you can't even understand that, can you? But, *man,* I am not scum. I will take you home, though I would rather just leave you here, on the side of the road, in the middle of nowhere.

Man, my brother, I'm really sorry that I made you feel blue, Hillel says. But truly, I'm not a right-wing person or anything like that, brother. I just want to live in an ecological, green environment, you know what I mean, man? Isn't that so, Renana?

Renana doesn't say anything.

Two years later, Sahar, aged twenty-six, goes to sleep and never wakes up. The funeral takes place in the kibbutz cemetery. We're heading back to Tel Aviv from the funeral in a friend's car. The Galilee landscape passes the car window through a curtained gaze. We cross the Jezreel Valley. From here, in our current state of matter, Jezreel Valley spreads in front of us and is made out of Lego.

From the car, in the light of the early afternoon, the little houses on the little hills are perceived as toys. The trees are toys. The cars, the clouds, everything made out of Lego. My girlfriend is staring at the clouds above Mount Gilboa and says, look, you could see the world moving.

What Jezreel Valley used to be for us has fallen and smashed to smithereens that gather in the billowing haze. And then, out of nowhere, come the horses; white and big, grazing The horses that are only puppets of horses.

THE RELUCTANT HOTELIERS: THE SCOTTISH HOTEL IN TIBERIAS

by Julia Handelman-Smith

When visiting my husband's family in Tiberias for Passover, a colleague urged me to stay at the Scots Hostel. Having lived in Israel for a few years, I had grown used to staying in many of the Holy Land's Christian hostels. Most of them offer simple, tranquil accommodation in some of the most historic locations. In this case, I must have missed the absent "s" and was quite unprepared for the experience.

What awaited us was Israel's 2008 Boutique Hotel of the Year. Situated on the bank of the Sea of Galilee, we were led through idyllic gardens to a large, cool room in the Doctor's House, one of the three original buildings of classic honey-coloured stone of the mid-nineteenth-century Ottoman Empire.

There seems to be little to connect this Middle Eastern paradise to Scotland apart from the Scottish flag flying from the garden tower and the odd bit of tartan in the hotel's Ceilidh Bar. However, the Scots Hotel started out as the Scottish Hospital, founded by Dr David Watt Torrance in 1894, and formed part of the Church of Scotland's extended mission in the Holy Land. The complex served as a fully functioning hospital, treating patients from as far away as Damascus, right up until the fledgling Israeli state opened its first hospital in the region in 1959.

Following that, the complex became a Christian guesthouse, offering accommodation for Christian visitors to the iconic sites of the Galilee, much like its sister institution in Jerusalem. However, come the late Nineties the buildings were crumbling and the meagre hostel fees stood no chance of covering the cost of its upkeep.

And so, after existing gracefully through Ottoman rule, Jewish settlement, Israeli independence and the subsequent Arab-Jewish wars, the Scottish mission in Tiberias entered into its most turbulent times when a £13million investment was approved for a boutique hotel. There are still those both within and outside the Church of Scotland that fervently oppose its ownership of a luxury hotel that primarily serves a wealthy Jewish clientele. Whilst the hotel does much to support local charities by providing reduced rates to local Christian groups and supporting the Church of Scotland's mission in the north of Israel, it seems that it has yet to fulfil its promise of providing revenues for the Church's wider mission overseas. The hotel hit the headlines once again last year as investment was approved for a wellness centre to keep up with the Joneses in the luxury hotel market. Many in the Church of Scotland feel that this business concern in Israel's territory is compromising its decisions in relation to the wider Israel-Palestine debate and missions.

However, any of us who have spent any time in the Holy Land understand that it doesn't take a luxury hotel to force you into the realm of compromise. Religious missions in the Holy Land started to make compromises from the moment they arrive, and I can't help feeling that the real and concrete challenges of running a viable business in Israel could only make the Church stronger in its understanding of the Galilee and its communities. As social enterprise becomes the new buzzword, I sense that the Church will become more comfortable with its luxury hotel.

Easter morning falls during Passover, and we wandered across the road to the small Scottish church for the Easter service. This is very much off-season for the Galilee–serious pilgrims are in Jerusalem–and so there were five of us, including the minister and his wife. This did not deter the enthusiastic and welcoming minister from demanding full participation.

For the guidebook part, the place is paradise. The gardens approach the biblical as you wander through pomegranate and hibiscus groves. The rooms are airy, cool and luxurious. The staff is diverse, and exceptionally welcoming and helpful. The breakfast is non-kosher and divine.

As I dropped a meagre twenty shekels into the offering plate in the Church, I thought about the two hundred quid I'd blown on our accommodation and realised it's the largest single contribution I've ever made to the Church. If you're weary after a series of worthy but basic hostels in the Holy Land, give yourself a treat–you will be supporting one of the few inclusive and politically neutral enterprises in the Galilee, and you'll have a wonderful time.

BETWEEN THREE NORTHERN CITIES
by Ron Levy-Arie

HAIFA: CAPITAL OF THE NORTH

Haifa is an interesting place. Well, for me as a person growing up on the dirty pavements of Tel Aviv, Haifa was not really love at first sight. It is unique and sometimes boring, multicultural yet slightly divided, outstandingly beautiful but grim, new mixed with ancient–it is the "Capital of the North", only an hour away from Tel Aviv, yet still it is a place with its own special character. A few months ago, we went to hang my wife's artworks at a gallery of our friends called HaMirpeset, meaning the veranda or the porch. We drove that same evening through one of the most casual residential streets in the middle of town on our way to the Hadar neighbourhood–when suddenly we saw a nine-hundred-pound wild boar crossing the road. We closed the car's windows, pressed the gas pedal hard, and drove away from the spot with great panic mixed with excitement. We turned on the radio to hear if there were any reports of a boar running wild with vengeance in the rural streets of Haifa–but there were none. We made it to the gallery and started telling our friends of our brave encounter with that big, fat beast, expecting to hear them praise us for our courageous experience–but they were as apathetic about it as if you told a New Yorker that you saw a squirrel in Central Park. Giving us the classic: "Oh, we get it all the time"–Haifa folks are special.

On the art front, Haifa does not stop surprising, with more and more artists appearing in several fields, like the crew of street artists that go by the name of Broken Fingaz. This crew pretty much reinvented Haifa in the mid-Noughties. They started out as a crew of graffiti artists who covered the inner streets of Haifa with their own special touch. Their favourite topics and imagery are big fat yellow men, sexual scenes between horny skeletons and seductive pink and purplish women, a touch of occult symbology, American billboards aesthetics and, yeah, wild boars and beasts. The crew widened its activity to being party promoters, fashion designers, musicians and DJs, and nowadays members of the Broken Fingaz extended family have shows, exhibitions and art displays worldwide. There are also bands like 3421, artists like Tant, Unga, Kip & Deso, and the talented Miss Red, who tours with UK producer The Bug. Not forgetting Easy, who are artists, MCs, a soundsystem and more. You can say that this scene today mainly revolves around HaMirpeset

Hadar was a proper downtown kind of place, with junkies and a poor population of shady characters and other *les misérables*. The place bloomed in the Sixties, but somehow it had been forgotten until the people from HaMirpeset came and started doing art exhibitions, parties, live shows and happenings, and rejuvenated the place. Actually, Hadar is right down below a street called Masada, which is known as the "young people" street in Haifa, with hipster cafés and some great early works by Broken Fingaz covering some of the walls.

Now the question many people ask is: Why Haifa? (And there are a lot more artists apart from the shortlist above.)

Some claim that the main talent competition is between Jerusalem and Tel Aviv. There is an old saying in Hebrew, "two quarrel, and the third wins"–and Haifa is obviously the third in this equation. People also attribute the special character of Haifa to the chemical refinery chimneys that pollute the air of this beautiful town located on Mount Carmel, overlooking the tranquil Mediterranean Sea. Or maybe it's because Haifa is a natural cosmopolitan place with Muslims, Christians, Jews and members of the Bahá'i religion living side by side in a sort of harmony.

Haifa was originally a "workers' town", with people working at the Haifa Harbour (which is still the main harbour in Israel) and in different factories in the city, and maybe there are still relics here of its old socialist atmosphere that makes people more inclined towards sharing and caring. You genuinely feel it–Haifa is less standoffish than Tel Aviv, maybe because people in Haifa don't try to constantly convince themselves that they live in the centre of the world, a feeling that Tel Avivians tend to have slightly too much. Therefore, Haifa is blessed with a certain humbleness–pretty much the opposite to Tel Aviv's arrogance.

And if I have to sum it up, and if you're already in the northern part of Israel–Haifa is a must. It's easy to get to – about an hour train ride from Tel Aviv. The train station is located at the foot of the mountain on which Haifa is built. There is the lower city (in Hebrew, "Hair HaTachtit"), with all the authentic restaurants you can find–some wonderful Arab restaurants and shawarma places. As you climb up you'll see the Bahá'i Temple, surrounded by the most beautifully attended gardens–you might even say that it is the Israeli version of the Taj Mahal. The Bahá'i are really cool people–the faith originated in Persia and it feels like a harmonious, monotheistic mix of Islam and Hinduism. You can also take a grand tour of the Temple before 4pm. The Haifa Museum of Art, with its changing exhibitions, is also worth checking out. You'll find some more galleries downtown, because they keep opening up. In addition, if you want some live indie shows, the hottest place right now is Syrup, which has a vibrant scene on the rise with many live performances coming from Tel Aviv merged with bands from the local scene—imagine that Tel Aviv is the village-sized version of London and Haifa is like Manchester in her glory years. Moreover, if Haifa's city life is getting too intense and you wish to wash off your hangover at the beach, you can always go to Hof Hakshatot, south of Hof Hacarmel.

AKKO: CITY OF MANY LAYERS

Akko (or in English, Acre), like Jerusalem, is a city of many layers, both historically and culturally speaking.

Historically, the city offers a glimpse of the cave of the crusaders, otherwise known as the Templars' Tunnel. It's always fascinating to think about what is underneath the surface of a place and penetrate this underworld for a better understanding of the city as a whole. Like in Paris, where you have the catacombs, and under Jerusalem, where you can take a tour of the chain of caves that are dug under the Old City, Akko has its own set of caves to be proud of. The tunnels' restoration started in 1994, and they were only opened to the public relatively recently in 2007—and they are really worth a visit.

The old market is also an enchanting place, where you can see all the herbs and spices from the Galilee Mountains and fish that you can only get up north. The hummus that you find in the heart of the market at Sa'eed is considered to be some of the best in the whole country, and the stall

Entrance to the Echo Chamber

Tsfat cheese

The Hebrew calendar on a wall in the Old City

is open only until noon. It is like heaven for hummus fanatics–creamy like Italian mascarpone and hardly spiced with any extras, a real treat for foodies. When you finish licking your fingers and you feel like having a dessert, don't you dare miss the cnaff'e available around the corner–it's an ultra-sweet delight made with the tiniest macaroni and special goat's cheese sweetened with aromatic sugar waters. Have that with some fine Arabic coffee and you're the happiest camper alive.

In English they call the city Acre for some reason; we just call the place Akko, and please do the same when you get to Israel. It has been around for a good four thousand years, so when it comes to history, it's the place to go. If you're into early Christianity, Roman and Greek history, Jewish history from the rabbinical perspective, crusaders, early Islam or Napoleon Bonaparte you should never think about skipping Akko.

One of the city's main attractions is the annual Israel Fringe Festival. Imagine all these twelfth-century buildings with heavy stones and arches filled with the most cutting-edge and obscure yet tasteful live theatre, and hundreds of performers filling the ancient streets of the city, with actors and shows from across the country and worldwide. The festival usually takes place in September, but it is best to check online. Many of the shows are co-productions between the local community and directors and different artists from varying performance fields, which can create fascinating combinations and even helps to build a cultural bridge that binds the many gaps we tend to have in Israeli society. The Festival started in 1980, and you might say that now it's one of the most important cultural attractions in the country. But if the Festival is not on when you visit, then there is the Akko Theatre Centre, established in 1985, which has a fully active year-round artistic programme that intermingles Arab and Israeli artists with off-centre plays and postmodern theatre–things that are even hard to find in Tel Aviv.

There's also a very famous restaurant called Uri Buri that is considered one of the finest fish restaurants in the country–it is best to book a table before, since the place is always jam-packed. They know what they are worth, and it might not be the cheapest experience, but it is certainly worth it. Akko in a way is like being in Jerusalem with a sea, which maybe is the greatest difference that there could be–Jerusalem is a mystical fortress surrounded by mountains, but you can't throw a fisherman's net and catch your dinner. Akko is in the middle of the Mediterranean Sea, and the sea breeze balances it and makes it a more peaceful place–I guess that geography affects people and their political agenda. Let's not forget that throughout the years Akko has been conquered by any conqueror worth his salt. But after years of wars, bloodshed and conquest, Akko can now start moving towards a better future.

TVERYAH: THE GOSPEL ROAD

Let's face it, Tiberias (or as we say in Israel, "Tveryah") is a has-been kind of town–a town with a glorious past and an uncertain future. But the setting is a killer when it comes to beauty. It's a dozy little town on the banks of the Sea of Galilee. But when saying "Sea", let's tell the honest truth, it's not really a sea–it's a medium-sized lake, or a very small one compared to Lake Michigan, that is the source of most of the drinking water in Israel.

Today's Tveryah has a highly orthodox Jewish population living in a place that was once a great tourist attraction. A few decades ago, Tveryah was a popular tourist destination for

Yirmiyahu and me

So where does all the magic happen?

Rabbi Yosef Karo Synagog

both local and international holidaymakers that gave them the full "Israeli experience"–holy places, a beach and fried fish. In other words, an awkward combination of Jerusalem and Palm Springs. Tveryah is one of the four holy cities of Judaism. It was the place where the *Mishna* was written (one of the most significant texts in Jewish studies) and where the Sanhedrin (the Jewish court of law) was formed back in the third century. It is also home to many tombs of the main figures of the Jewish world, like those of the "Rambam", Rabbi Mei'r Baal Ha'nes, and others. People gather from all over the world to pray to the tombs while lighting a candle for their virgin daughter or for better welfare for their family, for health, strength and encouragement. Some call it "Jewish voodoo", and some say it's just part of the tradition.

Tveryah is also the cradle of Christianity, the dwelling place of Jesus Christ and his disciples. Here is where he fed the five thousand with only five loaves of bread and two fish–and don't you dare call JC stingy, because back in the day it was the best meal in town. My wife and I went to the very church where it is written to have taken place, which is called Tabgha, a very modest chapel compared to the spectacular churches you'll find in Jerusalem. It's pretty much a souvenir shop with a designed fountain at the entrance with a few huge Chinese goldfish swimming in it. Funny thing is that the fish were the friendliest fish that we had ever met. They were as friendly as poodles. One particular fish was so friendly, he kept getting his little fish nose out of the water wanting us to pet him as if he was a little dolphin. I imagine that if all the fish had acted this way before the feeding of the five thousand, probably most of the folks would have said, "Let's skip the fish; I'll do just fine with a piece of bread. You know what, skip the bread–I'll give it to the fish, he seems kinda hungry." The beautiful thing about this church specifically is that the interior is quite minimalistic. In the stained-glass artworks in most churches one finds mainly figurative imagery, but in Tabgha it's all abstract, and its illuminated wall decorations can seem like clouds, mist, smoke, judgment day or a Rorschach test. And that raises some questions about the divine deity. These images don't show the story of the feeding of the five thousand–it's as if they're saying: "Everything is open to interpretation."

If you came all the way to Tveryah to grasp some of the living history of JC in order to get some spirituality, you might find it between a gift shop and abstract stained glass windows in a humble church, and I kinda like that concept. I asked the housekeeper at Tabgha if she knows a way to get to the seashore from the church. She said, "Yeah, just walk up the road to the hidden fountain." We took the car, and I guess it was so hidden that we missed it (it's supposed to be a nice place, though). Instead, we found ourselves walking in a beautiful grove leading us to the sea. I said to my wife, "It reminds me of northern Jamaica." Apparently, it was St Peter's church. It is truly a peaceful place with access to the seashore, or lakeshore to be exact. We spent some time there reflecting.

As I looked over my shoulder, still wondering if I was in Jamaica for a moment, I saw a Rastaman walking with a group of pilgrims. I approached him and greeted him. He kindly answered me and a fascinating conversation developed. He was originally from Jamaica and we had many mutual friends and acquaintances, so we both started shooting the breeze in patois. He was a singer-songwriter and wrote a very famous song, and other songs by him are collector's items. I hooked him up with a music producer from Tzfat and felt there was something mystical about how

The Rastaman

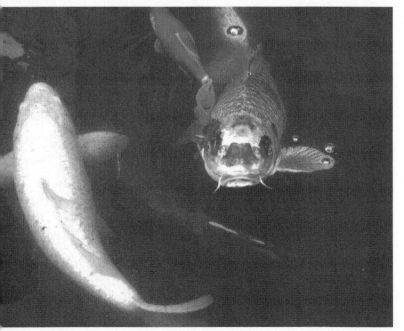

Hungry fish at Tabgha

these things came together, and how people from different cultures can find a common language after all on the banks of the Sea of Galilee.

PART FOUR: NEGEB

(Negeb, or Timna, is the southern desert, meaning "south" in ancient Hebrew. Janub in Arabic.)

A PATCHWORK CITY
— THE STORY OF BEERSHEBA

by David Sorotzkin
(Translated by Eilam Wolman)

How might one define Beersheba? A patchwork city. Like a jigsaw puzzle full of negative spaces that were gradually filled by parts of other puzzles, made of dozens of other puzzles. An urban jumble shaped primarily by a disinclination to remember, the desire to obliterate at any cost, with the residents seeming to move through the town's different parts out of a persistent, insatiable flight instinct.

Modern Beersheba was built in the beginning of the twentieth century as an Ottoman county town with a modern grid structure. Wide, crisscrossing streets of Arabian-style houses made of yellow desert sandstone, with arched windows, courtyards, and extensive entrances. The city was meant to assist the Turkish–and later the British–authorities in supervising over the Bedouin population, which stretched over the entire Negev and was uneager to submit to the rule of any central administration.

In the early Fifties, the Zionist leadership of Beersheba adopted an urban plan called the garden city movement, a blueprint for working-class cities conceived at the end of the nineteenth century by philosopher Ebenezer Howard and adopted both throughout various cities around the world and in Israel. This plan divided Beersheba into neighbourhoods with large open spaces between them. Every neighbourhood was meant to provide for its own needs. In each one, an urban centre was set up with shops, kiosks, and in some cases, a movie theatre. The original plan was for green vegetation to grow all over the neighbourhoods.

The consensus is that the garden city plan has failed. The neighbourhood gardens remain barren. The wide stretches between each section became wastelands crossing the geometric neighbourhoods. The neighbourhoods were filled with working-class homes, inhabited mostly by Oriental Jews, and built in line with the visions of socialist construction characteristic of Israel in its first decades. Public housing projects, or "blocks", as we called them, with tiny units for the emerging Israeli proletariat, made up of new immigrants. With these engineered urban spaces, the ruling party controlled the peripheries from its Tel Aviv and Jerusalem offices.

The new neighbourhoods sprung up north of the original Turkish centre, called the Old City for the stark contrast between its housing style and that of the more recent architectural projects. The immense empty spaces between the neighbourhoods were quickly overrun with insects, turtles and porcupines. As a child, I would come down from our apartment building and follow swarms of beetles and worms around for hours on end.

The planning of Beersheba was the old elite's response to a conflict with the local Bedouin population. In a different way, it was also a response to a conflict with the new, mostly north African immigrants. David Tuviyahu, Beersheba's first mayor, gave the city its character, and renowned architect and city planner Arieh Sharon drafted its urban outline. The new neighbourhoods were built as an antithesis to the Old City, which represented the Arabic and Levantine elements that the new Israelis of the Fifties and Sixties wished to distance themselves from.

Until the end of the Eighties, the Old City functioned as Downtown Beersheba, the floundering shopping area where everything was sold from haberdashery and food to clothes and hats. From the early Eighties onwards it was badly neglected, and after an abortive attempt to develop and make it into an artists' quarter–an initiative that resembled such restoration programs as in Jaffa, Acre and other Arabic towns–the Old City sank into decay. The Jewish population, which consisted mostly of Orthodox and other observant groups, was forsaking it for newer neighbourhoods and other cities: Bnei Brak, Ashdod and Jerusalem.

During the Nineties, with the collapse of many of the city's older businesses, the state began settling Palestinian collaborators from the occupied territories in the Old City, and it was soon filled with brothels, gambling houses, junkies and migrant workers. In recent years, there's been a change of direction. The Arabian architectural style became an attraction. The Old City is in great demand. Assets are few and prices are rising. Beersheba is giving students property tax discounts so that they would settle in the area, and various associations devoted to "Jewifying" the Negev and the Galilee are acquiring houses in it.

As early as Jewish Beersheba's first decades, Bedouin presence was distanced from the Old City as part of the subjugation and Jewification of the territory. Many transformations were imposed on the traditional Bedouin markets, which included livestock, clothes and rug markets, in order to distance them from the Jewish areas. At the level of regional geographic and demographic planning, the Bedouins, who dominated the entire Negev up until 1948, were now concentrated in a narrow geographic triangle–like the Pale of Settlement designated for Jews in imperial Russia–between Beit Kama, Arad and Dimona. The Bedouins' land was confiscated by the state, which to this day continues to claim there is no proof that it belonged to them. The Bedouins themselves were forced into semi-desolate permanent settlements and entirely desolate piratic settlements without water or electricity. Being a very non-compliant group with an aversion to authority, some of them have turned to the twilight zone of protection businesses, burglary, drugs and "illegal"–at least in the eyes of the state–settlement.

As a child, my father would take me to Bedouin areas that were still somewhere between nomadic tent encampments and temporary settlements of rickety tin shacks. The head of the family would sit in the central tent and receive his guests. During each visit, I would straddle one of the donkeys and journey the endless, open territory with a wooden rod in my hand. I'll never forget these jaunts, the evening light, the desert soil spreading everywhere in yellow-brown colours. Meanwhile a lamb would be slaughtered, and blood came flowing from its neck in a long, black stream. Two hours later, we would feast on the wonderful Bedouin mansaf in the tent–slices of lamb and rye served on a bed of thin pittas.

During that period, the late Seventies and early Eighties, the remaining migrating Bedouins settled in the outskirts of Beersheba's then-nascent southern industrial area, with the paradoxical name Emek Sara ("The Valley of Sarah")–perhaps the same desert to which Hagar, according to the biblical story, fled from her mistress Sarah. Today, many of them are still living in impoverishment, in what the state calls "illegal settlements", between this area and where most of Israel's chemical waste is handled, south of industrial area Ramat Hovav. Every time rockets from Gaza are fired at

Israel, some are intercepted above the skies of the familiar cities, and some are allowed to fall in "open areas". Only recently, two Bedouin men, two girls and a baby were mortally wounded following such falls in "open areas". The state insists that it will continue to refrain from shielding unrecognised settlements.

The new neighbourhoods of Beersheba were given the names of Hebrew letters: Neighbourhood Alef (A), followed by Beit (B), Gimmel (C), Dalet (D) and so on. Shikun Darom (south housing) was erected on the ruins of a transit camp south of the Old City. Shikun Darom, and Beersheba's northernmost neighbourhood, Dalet, became the roughest neighbourhoods in town. In the Seventies and Eighties, Dalet Tsafon (north) Neighbourhood, which we called "North Dallas", was known as one of the roughest neighbourhoods in Israel. Hordes of junkies hung around there, and grenades casually tossed into balconies were a common sight. We would meet the neighbourhood youth around the pubs of the Old City. Some of them kept razorblade halves under their tongues, which they would draw during brawls to carve "lines" in their adversaries: the lifetime memento of a long and ugly gash.

Between these two neighbourhoods, new ones were being built, which later came to be perceived in the local bourgeois jargon as "islands of sanity". The first among them, built in the early Sixties, was Hei Ledugma, modelled on the Carpet Settlement, which consisted of single-floor patios connected to each other by paths. Next to it was the "quarter kilometre block", inspired by Le Corbusier, which became a hotbed of crime and drugs. Contrary to plan, the socialist housing of Hei Ledugma became an attraction for the sated Beersheba bourgeoisie. More bourgeois neighbourhoods were built in the following decades, such as Rasco City near the Old City in the south, and Vilot Metsada ("Masada Villas") up north, not far from the crime scenes of Dalet.

Following the founding of these neighbourhoods, the middle class began leaving in droves for satellite settlements Omer, Lehavim and Meitar, homogeneous villa suburbs that provided their residents with high living standards and, most importantly, distanced them from the rest of the Beersheba population and their derelict houses. By the beginning of the Nineties, Beersheba consisted of neighbourhood islands, each surrounded by the wilderness of the collapsed Garden City: the carcass of a socialist vision that never took shape.

In 1972, after a number of setbacks, the current Beersheba City Hall building was erected near the centre of town, on the main road that crosses the length of the city. A flat cement structure engraved with horizontal lines that veil narrow windows, with a tall tower from its front to its left reminiscent of the torch held aloft by Lady Liberty, City Hall is located next to what was once Cinema Keren–Beersheba's largest auditorium, built in the Fifties and demolished in the Nineties–and not far from Beit Ha'am ("House of the People"). Both were quality modernist structures, singular in the city, inclined with straight, clean lines. Beit Ha'am, similar to the Culture Palace in Tel Aviv but smaller, was home to the Beersheba Theatre, where various films played every afternoon. My father was among the theatre's founders, and as a child I saw many movies there. One of them was *Planet of the Apes*, and its final scene is etched in my mind forever. Charlton Heston standing on the beach, facing what's left of the head and torch of the Statue of Liberty as it is being submerged by the sand. His hope to flee the doomed planet crashes before his eyes. The place from which he'd hoped to escape is the very place he aspired to reach. The freedom of the future is engulfed in the sands of the past. In various stages of my tangled relationship with Beersheba, my plans to escape it alongside its reappearance at the edge of my life's tunnel, I had similar feelings towards the city; as if my future was leading nowhere but to the past, in ideal cyclic motion which resembles the idea of Chris Marker's featurette *La Jetée*.

During my early childhood, my father was Beersheba's deputy mayor. I spent many hours in the municipal building where his office was. As a small child, I walked around the straight and dark hallways made of bricks and concrete, charmed by the mysterious structure and its insinuated secrets. One day, as I was walking down one of the hallways, a man suddenly appeared and drew a handkerchief out of nowhere. The handkerchief in his hand quickly became a rabbit, and immediately afterwards he laid it on my hand and pulled it again, leaving in its wake many pieces of a spongy substance that miraculously reassembled into one complete sponge. It was Meir Buyom, the legendary magician of Beersheba, who worked in maintenance at the City Hall during the day and concocted his magic tricks by night. Spellbound, I began following him around in all of my many visits to City Hall until I became his shadow.

In my childhood memories, Buyom's magic merged with the municipal offices' dim corridors, leading into each other as in an ideal rectangular prison, going around and around, and with the no-man's-land of Garden City that surrounds the City Hall, barren areas where the desert left its bite marks. Neighbourhoods and desert, round and round. And beyond this, virginal industrial areas divided by mixtures of tin shacks and Bedouin tent encampments. If man is "nothing but the image of his native landscape", such are my landscapes and images: cement mixing with tin and sand, and the primal, suffocating pain.

The stages of maturation and disillusionment from the enchanted realms of childhood resemble the processes of rationalisation circumscribed by Max Weber with the term "the iron cage". Initial enchantment is followed by the "saint's cloak" of strict rules, and then by the "iron cage", which is made lengthwise and crosswise, just like the city, and which encases our lives with a grip of steel. In this journey, we abandon the enchanted days of childhood, in which we've been poured into the world, and become barren structures ourselves. Most of us still remain trapped in an early sphere where the magic cycle that surrounded us is enclosed by square and rectangular cage structures. The faraway dream remains trapped in a shell which itself became a dream. Open spaces between heatwave, stricken tenement islands. The indigested remains of our real, severed lives, surrounded by barbed wire fences.

With the collapse of the Soviet bloc and the wave of Russian immigration to Israel, the face of Beersheba was transformed completely. A "development momentum" was set in motion to settle the tens of thousands of new olim (immigrants to Israel). This was mixed with intersections of capital and power, as well as more than a dash of contractor interests. The empty spaces that remained from the Garden City skeleton were quickly occupied with high-rises. Gardens were wiped out, old buildings were demolished and the residents seemed relieved to finally see the mound of memories from the city that never was sinking into oblivion.

Anyone who enters Beersheba now would hardly recognise the city it used to be. Patches over patches of precariously and incidentally related structures, meant only to fill empty urban spaces, and perhaps a large void felt by the residents. The development momentum which suffocated the city also eliminated its urban centres. From the end of the Eighties, shopping malls were built in their stead, and more recently shopping centres have opened in the eastern outskirts of town as well, near the old road to Hebron. The residents work, sleep and shop, because that's what there is to do in Beersheba, just let life pass; in the Israeli periphery at the turn of the twenty-first century, in the rubble of our childhood, in the ruins of our primordial Garden City.

ISRAELI TEXTILE — THE MORNING KITAN FACTORY IN DIMONA WAS CLOSED

by Roy "Chicky" Arad
(Translated by Ithamar Handelman-Smith)

Hananiah Ohayon, who worked at the factory for thirty-
two years,
The union chairman,
On the other side of the fence, beyond the gate,
Wearing a dark green tracksuit and a black kippah,
He refuses to open
Neither for me nor for anyone else. The rusty lock is
wrapped on the gate.
Orange cardboard signs spelling "let us finish with dignity"
on its side
And a garden of dying hibiscus.
"It's a disgrace," he tells me,
"The management has sent us a tabulation
I've got nothing to lose,
There will be blood."
Yesterday,
When he realised that everyone is getting fired, he locked
himself inside
The factory
And slept there with four co-workers.
They were the last ones to stay and fight.

He slept in the guarding booth where he used to work,
The other four slept in inner rooms
Where it's warmer.
When it was freezing in the morning, they burned some
charcoal for heat.
He tells me
That they are demanding to be compensated
For 170% of their wage,
Like it was in Kitan Nazareth,
But they are willing to compromise on 150%.
The company is only willing to give them 120%.
We're only talking about fifteen employees on the payroll
And the monetary difference of a few hundred thousand
shekels
But for that the employees it's a matter of principle,
A matter of pride,
Anything less than 150% and we're like slaves.
It is a pride that sparkled too late,
After years of being put down,
After years of pay cuts,
After years of sacking and sacking and sacking,
After years of silence,
Years of letting them walk all over
You.
"I was once a sportsman
I was a footballer in Hapoel Ofakim. I was a chief mechanical
engineer.
I became a cripple because of work,
And I've been guarding the entrance ever since."
Jenya Sulver,
Twenty-two years in the factory. Quality control.
Began working within a month of immigrating to Israel
from Ukraine.

"Straight to Dimona,
Straight to Kitan factory
It was hard from the beginning, but I loved the factory.
But I loved the people
I never thought they'd treat me like
That.
A year ago they labelled me "employee of the year" in *Yedioth Ahronoth* newspaper.
There was a photo of me then in
Yedioth Ahronoth.
When there were thirty-six employees left,
They said that we were the best.
What do we want?
We only want to be let go in a respectful manner."
The factory is at 1 Herzel Street, Dimona
It was purchased a few years ago, by Len Blavatnik.
Though the workers aren't at all sure
If Len Blavatnik is still the owner.
"He's in the USA,
He didn't even send us any of his representatives,"
Says Jenya. She's fifty-seven years old. "We've never seen him.
"When we asked the CEO to put us in touch with the representatives,
She said 'I am the representatives'."
Jenya's daughter, Yelena, is a secretary at a law firm.
She is dressed elegantly
And has come to ensure that her mother
Doesn't immolate herself,
Which Jenya has threatened to do here and there.
The fence is barricaded by tires.
Moisture of gasoline has already been cast upon them
And it blackens even further the black colour of the tires.
"I'm proud of my mother," says the daughter,

"Some people only talk but are afraid to fight.
My mother knows no other life than working at the Kitan factory,
She's not here only for the sake of it."
"The management that was hired doesn't care about textile, only figures,"
Says Jenya, "From the first day that the new CEO set foot here,
There has been a bad luck in the factory.
They told us that they'll only cut a little bit here
And things would get better.
These days everything is manufactured in China or Turkey.
 They ship it in containers
And then brandit Kitan
What do I want?
Well, I'm just looking for a respectful way to close the factory."
I ask her about the general elections next month and she replies:
 "Netanyahu and Lieberman are a strong couple.
Everything they say about Lieberman is wrong.
Everything they say about him is because they are afraid of him.
He's trustworthy and takes care of the people.
He'd come to this factory if it weren't for those
Troubles he is having."
And then the mayor arrives.
He's about to leave his office soon,
And become a member of parliament in a party led by a former TV star
And columnist, the son of another former member of parliament,
Columnist and TV star as well.

The mayor also blames the factory's CEO,
He has a soothing and pleasant voice,
"I told you so. I told that this girl always wanted
To close this factory."
The mayor calls the chairman of the Histadrut,
Israel's biggest trade union,
Hananiah complains he hasn't shown enough support.
Afterwards the mayor says "I've spoken
With the
Chairman of the Histadrut."
Because they let the mayor into the factory
They let me in as well
Accidently, we're both a bit early.
The mayor's advisor is wearing a black suede jacket similar to the
One that I've got at home, though his jacket is cleaner. And
All the buttons are intact.
The factory is full of old posters:
A model partially covered by a blanket tagged with the slogan:
"Kitan–Get in bed with the real thing."
The model's leg has an odd tattoo.
A newspaper article announces the factory's closure.
It is glued to the wall with heaps of scotch tape
That creates a big transparent cross on the wall of Kitan.
"Those greedy pigs don't want to pay you
a fair share," the mayor tells the employees.
"Greedy bastards", says Ohayon "and we were naïve,
To allow them to sack so many people."
Hananiah Ohayon stands at the parking lot,
A broken textile hero,
A shiny tear runs down his cheek
And curls along the side of his nose,

When Armand Lankari arrives at the scene,
He is the leader of the Dead Sea factories union,
And the chairman of the local branch of the Likud party,
He is wearing a fancy watch and a pair of Prada sunglasses.
Arrives the deputy mayor, who is also responsible for the
City's welfare, with golden Ralph Lauren embroidery
On her jacket.
As I try and photograph the employees with my cellular
phone,
The deputy mayor jumps into the frame with her Ralph
Lauren and hugs
One of them. "I too am Kitan Dimona," she says.
"Unfortunately," the mayor says, "I already told the
employees two years
Ago to prepare for bad days.
The workers were too naïve and didn't realise
That they were up against
Cynics."
The mayor's advisor whispers to Hananiah
To start burning the tires now,
As the mayor is here
And then needs to move on.
But Hananiah refuses. They were aiming to start at 10
o'clock.
There's another one hour and a half. The mayor arrived too
early.
I start a conversation with Nissim Nagouker, sixty-one years
old. He
Became deaf in the factory due to years of noisy machinery.
Nissim, an emigrant from India, worked in the factory forty-
three years
But it's hard for us to talk, he can't hear
My questions and replies with irrelevant answers.

His name is written on a sign in the parking lot.
Inside the factory there's also Abraham Avishar, sixty-two
years old.
"I'm new here," he says jokingly
"I've only been working here for the last eleven-and-a-half
years
So I'm second-class kind of employee.
Paid by the hour on minimum wages.
But I was lucky to get overtime for working on Saturdays."
He says. Apparently, he often protested about being a second
Class employee,
But he's not complaining anymore. Anyway everybody is
fucked
They're going to sack them all, be it first or second class of
Employees.
He used to operate a forklift but injured his back,
So then he was put on a guard duty.
"I can't stand seeing more employees
 Leaving the factory with tears in their eyes.
At my age, what are my chances getting out of here
And compete with young kids who just got out of the army?
If I'm not willing to work on holidays
They'll say 'Go, it doesn't suit us.' And I have sons in the
army.
"Kitan just opened twenty-two new stores. They've got
money.
A father can't buy himself a few villas before feeding his
kids," says
Tzipi Hayon who has been sacked six months ago and she's
proud
To have discovered the compensation pay at Kitan Nazareth.
She is the one who have brought the one hundred and
seventy,

The woman who brought the one hundred and seventy.
Jenya recalls the day the factory had one-thousand-two-hundred employees
"Some came from Dimona, some from Hebron," she says
"We had a good life
We knew how to squeeze the good life out of our small salaries.
Right?
Didn't we have fun? Weren't we always happy?"
And Hananiah recalls the holiday
breaks to Eilat.
"We're on the fringe, nobody cares about us,
This is why nobody is coming
Because we're not the doctors
Or employees of the Dead Sea factories," says Hananiah Ohayon.
Armand from the Dead Sea factories is offended
And offers to bus over eighty of his own employees to show support.
But also says that they need to do it right and agree on the time.
"Where is the minister of the periphery?
All they ever did for us is close down the factories," says Hananiah.
We approach the deputy of Human Resources
Who was somehow able to sneak into the building despite the employee's
Siege.
Hananiah says that he must have cut through the fence.
Walking Kitan's yard, a ghost factory.
Useless buildings, a gigantic plastic bag that is carried by the wind.
But the deputy HR's office appears to be tidy

And even a secretary is here somehow.
When the deputy sees the reporters he turns pale and says,
"No comment."
Behind him, framed certificates and qualifications bearing
his name,
And on his side, a wall covered with a photograph of textile
workers.
It's a black-and-white photo but not the black-and-white
of the outside
But the black-and-white of a Photoshop.
Armand Lankri, a gentleman with a moustache,
He could have a bit of Hollywood look, if he had a gun on
his side,
He takes the deputy aside for a private conversation.
He knows everybody.
Later on, when we're back at the mess,
Lankri tells us that the Dead Sea factories workers bought
every year
Kitan's products in order to support the factory's workers,
"Every year Kitan always kept cutting their workforce.
It's the Chinese that breaks them and also, what's their
name,
The Palestinian cheap labour as well."
Armand passes on the HR deputy's offer
To meet later on this afternoon and to close things quietly.
"The deputy HR manager should call us," Jenya says furiously,
"You are in no position to negotiate." Armand explains
And tells them that this week he had a three-hour long
meeting with
The Secretary of Treasury, though they once had a row.
"Dimona is not Nazareth. Most of the employees already
agree with him.
And listen man,

Life is all about compromising."
"It's true, life is all about compromising," says Hananiah,
nods his
Head approvingly and offers Armand to join them in the
meeting.
And then comes a photographer from Channel 10
And asks when will they start burning the tires.
The employees are worried
That Armand's BMW will be damaged once the tires are lit
On fire and ask him to move the car.
And then, on Thursday, 9.50am, ten
Minutes before the time they had scheduled to start burning
the tires,
Someone's had enough and the tires are lit.
"I'm going to burn myself,"
Cries Jenya Sulver while running towards the
Flames in tears until one of the employees stop her.
I bring her a glass of water as she is crying.
Everybody is silent and nobody knows what to do next.
"I hope that the whole factory burns down," hissed another
employee
With a pierced nose.
Maybe she isn't an employee, I don't know.
In the beginning the fire is weak but it grows steadily and
it's smoky.
Two fire trucks are storming in
With their sirens on full blast
And stops in front of the workers, rattling.
It's few minutes after 10am when some photographers arrive
as well
And they are upset that nobody waited for them
As the workers lightened the fire before the time they've
arranged with

The press,
Nonetheless, their ponytails blowing in the wind, they photograph the
Workers crying and shouting and mumbling broken speeches
Down by the great smoke that obscures Kitan factory.
The pride of Israel's textile industry,
All the rides Sapir [4] took in his car!
All the rides Modai [5] took in his car!
All the ministers of trade and industry!
All the ribbon-cutting ceremonies!
All the grants!
Fifty-four years of industry!
The smoke of the Kitan factory is rising and darkening everything.
Hananiah Ohayon stands against the wind
Covered in a thick black devilish carcinogenic.
"You may be able to put out this fire,
But the fire in my heart will never die." Says Hananiah
To the firemen who approaches him in their yellow suits,
Of gigantic Lego soldiers.
I notice that on all the signs that the workers prepared with marker pens
Somebody added stickers of the
New Histadrut.
Curious locals start to arrive, to get a glimpse of the action.
"Wow, it looks like all Dimona's fire trucks are here,"
someone says
Excitedly.

---

[1] Pinchas Sapir, born Pinchas Kozlowski, 15 October 1906-12 August 1975, was Israel's Minister of Finance during the first decades following the country's founding.

[2] Yitzhak Moda'i, 17 January 1926-22 May 1998, was Israel's Minister of Finance from 1984-1986.

He has an earring in both ears.
And then Jenya faints
The glass of water that I gave her falls from her hand.
 It shatters on the flo
Or.
The flo
Or
Is all covered with shattered glass
It's becoming dangerous. Someone pours water on Jenya's
face
And she regains consciousness after a few minutes.
Everybody is surrounding her, I take a step back.
An ambulance arrives.
They place her on a wheelchair and start to move her
towards the
 Ambulance but she wakes up and demands to be released,
It's a fight for our home,
It's a struggle for 170% of the compensation but
We'll settle for 150%.
The fire is burning along
And one of the workers throws a plastic chair at the burning
flames.
Boom!
Jenya leans on the paramedic
And gets up from the wheelchair.
She rejoins the protest.
As the ambulance starts to leave
Jenya faints again in front of the Factory.
The ambulance hasn't left the parking lot yet and it returns
Only for Jenya.

THE SPICE ROUTE
by Ithamar Handelman-Smith
(Translated by Eilam Wolman)

"Whoever kills will get killed," a sandwich maker in Florentine once told me, swinging a cutting knife before my eyes.

A starred agama, thirty centimetres long, head large for its body, scales grey-brown like the desert, crawls on the asphalt. On the edge of Highway 40, a silver Toyota 4x4 Jeep is making its way from Mitzpe Ramon through the Alpaca Farm to the Wise Observatory. A large body of water is hovering on the horizon, a mirage, the sky's reflection in the hot air. You can see the agama on the road reflecting in the waters of the mirage. The Jeep passes the farm and turns right into a dirt road, delimited by two asymmetrical lines of bright, round, medium-sized stones. These serve as an aesthetic, psychical preface to the atmosphere that will soon prevail. At the edge of the long dirt road, the grounds become visible. Eight wooden cabins scattered on the sandy, rocky soil in deliberate disarray. The place is called A Caravan in the Desert, a kind of guesthouse. Mitzpe Ramon isn't far, about seven kilometres from here. The huts are simple cabins, similar to some of the ones you find in the half-island of Sinai. They're made from wood, cloth, nylon, a shading net and palm fronds. They have no cement foundations. The furnishing inside is sparse, the design incoherent; a mishmash of Bedouin elements with features recalling the Rainbow and Burning Man festivals. The Jeep parks next to Abraham's tent. The jazz quartet gets off. The four are now returning from their last concert at Hangar Adama, at the Mitzpe Ramon Poetry and Literature Festival.

The next morning, Uriah leaves his cabin and sits down on a low easy chair, a green canvas sheet stretched on white iron perches. The saxophone rests on his knees like a rifle. Three girls sit on the wooden bench between his hut and the one nearest his. They're also in a band, they're called Habanot Ruchama or something, and they played in the festival too. Uriah hasn't really spoken to them but he and the prettiest one of the three got to exchange a few not-innocent glances.

The prettiest one of the three is wearing plastic flip-flops the colours of the Brazilian flag and her toenails are painted deep red. Her pants are tight and very short and her legs are tanned and long. The little pot belly exposed by her sleeveless belly shirt conveys fierce sexuality. With her brown, long hair fluttering in a warm desert wind, she approaches Uriah and assumes an alluring position above him, her muscular legs spread over his easy chair.

"Yes," Uriah says. "Can I help you with anything?"

"I could see you staring at me all the time, at the Orly Castel-Bloom talk, and then the Yoram Kaniuk talk, before you and your friends went up to play. You couldn't take your eyes off me," she says.

"Let's, I…" he falters. "Let's assume that's true. What do we do about it?"

"I don't know. We're leaving today," she says and tosses a

glance at her friends, who return her a vague, knowing look.

"So are we," he says, and sits bolt upright on the low chair, his eyes meeting her deep navel.

"You're going back to Tel Aviv?"

"No, we're going up the spice route and then taking the Arabah road to Eilat and then to Sinai. You want to join?"

His eyes climb from her navel to the conical breasts under the thin top and then to her long neck and her round, pretty, intense face.

"I wish I could but I need to go back," she says, brings her legs back together and moves aside.

"Don't just go."

"Do you have another idea?" she says, seemingly uninterestedly.

"Hmm... you want to go for a walk?"

"I'm too hot."

"Let's take a shower then..." he says, lighting himself a rolled cigarette of hydroponic marijuana.

"You're not so shy after all, are you?" She takes a puff from his cigarette, scratches her chin to mime deliberation and then extends her hand to him.

"Let's go," she says, and they head to the communal showers area together.

An hour later, Uriah and his friends are on the road again. They go north towards Sde Boker and enter Avdat, to see the Nabatean antiques. Avdat is a central town on the Nabatean trade axis, which two thousand years ago stretched from Petra to the port of Gaza. The acropolis, the town centre of Avdat, stands at the side of the ancient axis, and spreads across the Negev mountains, reaching 2150ft above sea level. Once, the ancient Nabateans stood on the Avdat acropolis and worshipped Arabian mountain god Dushara or love goddess Al-Uzah. Now Uriah and his friends are standing there and smoking weed.

They're going back towards Mitzpe Ramon. The journey begins at the northern cliff. From the visitor centre on the cliff's edge they survey the entire crater. In the midday light of a tangerine October sun, a little after Sukkot, the crater looks like the view on the moon or on Mars. Afterwards, they proceed to the woodshop and to Wadi Ardon. On their way to the nature reserve, they stop at the side of the road to look at a male mountain goat standing on one of the low cliffs near the road and looking at them.

"Come on, let's move on," says Jack, the pianist, who is also the driver, thanks to his parents, who let him borrow their Toyota Rav Jeep. "I want to get to see some more Nabatean cities."

"What do you want with these Nabatean cities?" says Danny, the drummer, while rolling another spliff, this time with hash which had come all the way from Lebanon.

"People lived here in real cities for two thousand years or one thousand and five hundred years, like this, in the middle of the desert, with no air conditioning... you wouldn't last five minutes here without air conditioning."

"Who cares? Who were they again?" Danny asks, smoking the potent hash and coughing.

"Merchant tribes who journeyed from the half-island and traded all sorts of old goods, I don't know, silk, perfumes, spices..."

"Frankincense and myrrh," says Uriah.

"Where did you get that from?" Danny says, smiling.

"Anyway, what made them special was that they knew to survive in the desert and they could always find water in it. Picture a long procession of hundreds of camels crossing this desert on the way to the Gaza port, where they'd load the goods on ships that sailed to Egypt and Europe too. It's crazy, isn't it? Like, two thousand years ago…" Jack says. They don't stop for the whole way on Highway 40 towards the Arabah until they reach Highway 90, by Faran, and proceed from there to the ruins of Nabatean city Moa, the last one on the spice route before Jordanian Petra. The antiques there don't impress them as much but Jack reads every encyclopaedic entry he can find about them on his Galaxy smartphone. They turn around and drive towards Eilat. In the east, a twilight sun paints the mountains of Edom with a fervent colour, making them truly red.

"I'm hungry," Jack says.

"Me too," says Ronnie. Danny and Uriah are hungry as well. At the side of the road they notice signage to a nearby tavern, simply called The Spice Route. They turn to a side road leading to the place, a removed farm in the no man's land between Israel and Jordan.

A low wooden fence surrounds The Spice Route. The inn is made of wood too. The entrance door is like a swing door from Wild West saloons. Colourful "Spice Route Inn" signage hangs above it. The place is empty save for tall a man in his mid-fifties with broad chest and shoulders. His sunburnt face is ploughed with wrinkles and adorned with a black grey beard, loose, unclean. He's wearing a green cowboy hat and a buttoned plaid shirt, mostly red and green, worn jeans, pointed cowboy shoes. A familiar combination of a retired IDF combatant and an Israeli cowboy; a rather obsolete style.

"Hello," he greets them assertively.

"Hello, mister," says Uriah. "What do you have to eat?

The place looks closed."

"We're open and there's plenty of food," says the man. "Why don't you sit down, have some lemonade and beer and look at the menu?"

"Sure, I'm starving," Jack says, and the quartet sits on brown wooden benches at the foot of a large and long wooden table, in matching colours, in the centre of the restaurant.

"Great place you got here," Uriah tells the man "How did you get here?"

"I ran away from life," says the man. "I served in the military for thirty-five years. I was in Unit 101 and I was in the Paratroopers Brigade. Everybody here knows me and knows that you don't mess with Jeroboam Hanegbi."

"What does that mean?" Danny asks, and immediately adds, "Can I smoke?"

"Smoke as much as you want, it's your lungs. What does it mean that you don't mess with me? It means what it means. Would you all like the pesto ostrich steak?"

"Sounds good," Ronnie says,

"We'll go for it," the rest say unanimously, and Jeroboam Hanegbi begins to prepare the food on the counter before their eyes, swinging his butcher's knife.

"Did you come from Tel Aviv to travel?" he asks.

"Yeah. We performed in some festival in Mitzpe Ramon. Now we're heading to Eilat and Sinai."

"What festival?"

"Poetry and literature," says Danny.

"Nice. Eilat is great. But why Sinai? I don't visit Arab countries," Hanegbi says, slicing slabs of ostrich meat.

"What does that mean?" says Uriah, sipping his beer.

"It means what it means. You're probably leftist Tel Avivians, but I know things you guys don't know."

"Like what? You people always say that. But look at you, making your steaks with pesto and preaching these right-wing opinions... don't you think it's funny?" Jack says, moving his thin-framed optical glasses up and then down the bridge of his long, Jewish nose.

"What's funny about it, kid? What do you know about life anyway? I'll bet none of you even went to the army."

"So what?" says Uriah. "We believe in other things, man. We believe in peace and love, you know... think about Rabin, he was a soldier and a fighter and everything and didn't know anything outside of that life, and even he understood the importance of peace."

"Rabin? Ha..." Hanegbi grunts, now swinging the knife in his hand. "Rabin was a traitor, even back in the Altalena days, and the Bible says 'whoever kills will be killed', it is written."

"Where does it say that, can you show us?" Ronnie laughs.

"Yeah, where?" says Jack. "You just made that up the same way you'd made up your entire funny existence over here, in this hole..." he says and bursts into laughter. The others join him and now the four of them are mooing with bellowing laughter. At first, they don't even see Jeroboam Hanegbi pulling out his old M1 carbine. The thunder of the first shot will petrify them. White-red slivers of Uriah's brain will scatter all over the table, the bench and the exposed floor. The others won't be spared. Hanegbi will shoot everywhere and empty a full magazine of thirty 0.3-inch bullets on them. Horrified and screaming, they will try to escape, hide under the table and behind the benches, but to no avail. Danny will catch five bullets in different areas of his body but the last one will hit the neck, splay copious blood and finally kill him. Ronnie and Jack will crawl on the floor bleeding, leaving a long and dark trail of blood in their wake. Hanegbi will stand above them and shoot them in the back. Blood puddles everywhere. Hanegbi will confirm the kill with a bullet from zero range to the head of each of his young victims.

DREAMERS UNDER THE SUN
by Sagi Benita (Translated by Eilam Wolman)

Under a cowboy-hat-shaped monument by the southern sea shore, an engraving reads:

> God's Neshama Yeseira belonged to Nelson Raphael. The man who never did a thing he could put off to the next day. The man who saw with one eye what others couldn't see with two. The man who put beer and humor first. The man who put Eilat on the sea as well as on the map.

He had lost an eye in the battle of Malkia in the Galilee, and with his black beard and the cowboy hat he never took off had the appearance of some British admiral called Nelson who lived in the eighteenth century and lost his eye in Corsica. Nelson owned a resort village on the Taba border. The women travellers there were always naked. The strong sun was washed down with beer. Food was foraged from the sea, and the heady herbs were imported from Sinai. People ate with their hands, made love with other organs, danced with ecstasy up the mountain by the golden calf, and sang Ray Charles with all their hearts. The only doctrine preached was the village's slogan: "Every day is a holiday."

Eilat is an autonomous state of mind, separate from other parts of the land–not only because of its geographic isolation and the combination of the gulf and the mountains. It's the only resort town bordering two Arab states, Jordan and Egypt. Nelson passed on in 1988, and a year later, Israel returned Taba to Egypt, and the village went with it.

The generation born in the Seventies would come to embody Rafi Nelson's Neshama Yeseira. Wild beach kids, drinkers and voluptuaries, taking everything the generous little piece of the sea had to offer: tourists, roasted fish, cheap beers.

When we were kids, we would fantasise that one day, oil reserves would be discovered in the Eilat Mountains, or gold would be found in the mines of the Timna Valley, and we could live off the dividends and never work. We believed one day we could swim to the glittering lights in Aqaba, row a small boat from Eilat to Jordan. Our lives were a mess of fact and fiction. Our dreams rotated on a spit of lassitude. "Don't do today what you can do the day after the next," as it were; except the day after the next became the year after the next. Years passed in staring at the Red Sea, nights in watching the mountains of Edom wearing the Aqaba lights like a diamond ring.

Eilat's ancient name was Etzion Gever, which was an ancient city in the land of Edom at the top of the gulf, near the Eilat and Aqaba of modern times. In the Bible, the children of Israel rest there after the exodus from Egypt. They must have known what we had felt in our bones since we were born in Eilat: Rest. There's nowhere to go. We are free. Some people call the Golan Heights up north the "eyes of the country". Eilat, the most southern city, must be Israel's lazy feet. It's so hot and arid you always end up dipping in the sea. If you've made it to Eilat, you know there's nowhere to go to from here. When there's nowhere to proceed towards, you withdraw inward and cross psychical continents, become a desert sage, an official spokesperson for the sea. We always dreamed of an avocational life. Destination is secondary. I'm only now realising what a great distance I'd travelled just to return to the seaside. The beach is freedom. The final destination. What *is* purpose? Where does it lead? Our lives became one long exemplary sunrise; first, an inwardly incandescent indolence, then, meaning spraying from everything.

THE ROAD TO EILAT: FROM THE DEAD SEA TO THE RED SEA

the ancient Arabah is a narrow valley, about ninety-nine miles long. It separates the mountains of Edom in the east from the Negev mountains in the west. Walking on the vaporous, reddish surfaces of the Edom mountains must be what walking on Mars feels like. You can always ponder weightless issues, disconnect from Earth's atmosphere, search for signs of new, alien lifeforms.

Life on Arabah kibbutzes has in fact taken on new, alien forms with time. Forty-three miles from Eilat, at the kibbutz of Neot Smadar in the southern Negev mountains, a mirage is revealed: next to a lake at the heart of the desert is a magnificent pink palace where people walk in silence. The kibbutz was founded in the late Nineties by academics from Jerusalem who had left the bloody tensions behind to create a community based on the philosophical ideas of Krishnamurti and Carlos Castaneda; the letting go of the past and removal of social conditioning. Wearing brand-name clothing is prohibited in Neot Smadar, as is the use of cellphones in public spaces. The economy is based on organic agriculture. The kibbutz motto is displayed on the dairy wall: "To effectively examine the secret of cooperation between people and create a learning community." I only sneaked in once, through the plum orchard. A gong sounded exactly when I got inside. All members of the kibbutz ceased their work and spent a long minute in awe of the moment. The place looked like heaven on Earth, but their spirit was trapped. Their redemption seemed to have imprisoned them. Like a scene out of *Invasion of the Body Snatchers*, their sensors had picked up on me and within less than ten minutes I was outflanked and kicked out. They did not learn a single thing about hospitality from either Krishnamurti or Castaneda. They did bring one miracle into being at the kibbutz. The best organic plum juice I'd ever had was at the Neot Smadar Inn, on the main road between Ramon Lookout and Eilat.

The testy intestines of our land have puked up many fanciful minds onto the arid Arabah. In the Fifties it was adventurous young men who were testing their own courage by trying to infiltrate Jordan and reach the red rock in Petra.

Beyond the mountains and the desert
So the legends have it
Is a place no one's returned from alive
And it is called the red, red, rock
– Haim Hefer

One of these adventurers was Shimon Rimon, whose nickname was "Kushi". In 1959, along with his friend Victor Friedman, Kushi crossed the border into Jordan with a Jeep and uniforms the two had stolen from the UN. Since the Fifties, Kushi had managed to get embroiled in drug deals in Germany and all manner of burglary and larceny due to his uninhibited penchant for adventure. He eventually chilled out and opened the Kushi Rimon Inn on the 101st kilometre. People on their way to Eilat had a tourist attraction waiting for them at the Inn–a zoological garden in the heart of the desert, including a two-headed snake, a two-headed turtle and a goat with six feet. In 2005, a fire consumed the zoological horror show. There are freaks that even nature won't tolerate.

In the Seventies, for the first time in Israel, a film city was built in the style of the Wild West, by Nahal Shlomo in Eilat. It all started when an Italian western, *Don Carlos*, was shot in Wadi Shahamon. The film crew stayed at the Caravan Hotel. By the end of the shoot, the production didn't have enough money left to pay for the hotel. It was decided that in return for the crew's stay, the farm that was built for the set would remain standing. A few years later, it went up in flames. The community leaders hired the same man who had constructed the set for the film, and the Texas Ranch Farm was built.

As we entered the Ranch, Ennio Morricone's desert harmonica was playing in our heads. A convoy of horses stood by the saloon. At the centre of town were a guillotine and hanging ropes. A thorn bush was rolling in the wind towards the prison by the sheriff's offices. Riding our horses up Nahal Shlomo, all we were missing to make the picture perfect were Indians, or enemies to fight. We never had enemies or wars. We fought the greatest enemy of all—boredom.

The climate and primeval scenery made Eilat and the Arabah an arable ground for film shoots. Breakthrough Israeli films like *Hole in the Moon*, popular comedies like *Israel Forever*, and big-budget American and British films were all shot there. At one point, a rumour started running around that the third movie in the *Rambo* series would be shot in the Timna Valley. The headlines in the local newspaper read: "English-speaking extras needed." We were thrilled and we brushed up on our English so we could get in the picture, but the requirements included a dark skin colour. We dreamed of Hollywood, unaware we would be playing the Afghan kids. Every ten-year-old in 1988 with a dark skin colour was accepted to play in the film. The ones whose skin was browner, like the Yemenites, received a hundred dollars a day. The rest had to settle for fifty and paint their skin with a black, greasy polish. Early in the morning, they drove us along with hundreds of other kids to Timna Valley. Next to Mangan River, an Afghan village was erected from the foundations up. We stood in the sun for twelve hours with the polish running down and stinging our eyes. Blasts kept going off, but Stallone never came to rescue us. We didn't even see him. Lunch included a juicy steak and fries. We gobbled it and drank cold Coke. It really was good. In the evening, they returned us to Eilat and paid us in dollars. It took me two hours to get the paint off my body. That's all I remember from being an Afghan child under Soviet rule.

THE RED CANYON
by Sagi Benita (Translated by Eilam Wolman)

Holding the promise of a serenity greater than the sea, the pristine Eilat mountains at the tip of the gulf are the crown of the desert's beauty, offering the widest variety of rocks in the country.

Hiking at the beautiful Red Canyon, only a twenty-minute drive from Eilat, is most suitable for both families and lovers. The canyon stands seven hundred metres above sea level and is therefore great for hiking in the summer, so long as it's done in the early morning and afternoon hours. In the winter, dress warm and be mindful of floods. Two circular trails are available to visitors: one is a kilometre-and-a-half long, the other four kilometres long. The long one is marked with red and begins at the parking lot. We will focus on the shortened trail and take Road 12, which leaves west of Eilat, towards Avdat village and Mitzpe Ramon. Let's go up the road, along the tops of the Eilat Mountains. Stop for a minute and take in the beautiful view of the gulf. Twenty kilometres later, signs appear with directions to the Red Canyon. We'll take a right to the dirt road and zigzag with it until it diverges in two. Proceed on the trail marked in green towards the canyon. The parking lot is four hundred metres from where the trails diverge, so just stay in the vehicle until you get there.

At the parking lot, a trail marked in green leads us into a

short creek, at the end of which we are spilled into a larger gully, called Wadi Shani. Another trail is marked in black. It would lead us up a path overlooking the same creek. At the very start of the road, you can see unique geologic phenomena such as sandstone, congealed layer by layer over hundreds of millions of years. Sandstone is a result of quartz grains agglutinating due to long weathering from igneous rocks such as granite. You can see yellowish chalk rocks encrypted with remnants of shell and fish skeleton fossils, formed back when the sea had wrapped the mountains of Eilat with reefs and corals. The floods that have passed through Wadi Shani notched the stone and created a narrow cleft in mesmerising red colour. The wonder begins when we get to the waterfall. The river gets narrower, the atmosphere more bucolic. The wind and the waters have colourfully sculpted the rock. Handles and banisters assist us as we descend into the viscera of the canyon. Take the time and appreciate the surrealistic formations of the slopes. They began forming millions of years ago, when the hard sandstone drifted in giant African rivers. After the area dried, iron oxides and other minerals created the red colour we see in the canyon. Part of the descent is done by sliding inside smooth Nubian sandstone. Be careful, place your hands at the sides of the wall and use your legs for support. Along the way, the observant may notice nimble cape hyraxes peeking from the rock clefts, or a flock of ibexes on a cliff. Ancient rock paintings also appear in the clefts. Some of the passages are very narrow and, in the days of old, the canyon's crevice was used as a tiger trap. Relax. The tigers are long extinct. However, tiger traces and dung are found every once in a while in the Arabah and Negev. At the end of the canyon segment of the trail, a path on the right goes above the canyon and returns to the earlier river. It's narrow,

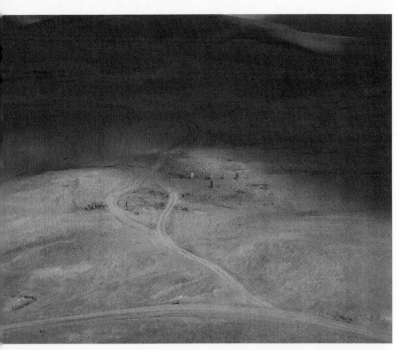

photographs by Assaf Shoshan (originally in colour)

Photographs by Assaf Shoshan (originally in colour)

somewhat frightening and not recommended for people with a fear of heights; they are advised to turn around and go back up the canyon. We'll return to the parking lot on the green trail. The hike takes ninety minutes, and is one-and-a-half kilometres in length. Bring water, comfortable walking shoes and a hat. Entrance is free, as it is on every trail in the Eilat Mountains Nature Reserve. Leave your cellular phone in the hotel room; there's no reception in the Red Canyon and on the Eilat mountains.

Photographs by Assaf Shoshan (originally in colour)

ICE CREAM VAN

by Ithamar Handelman-Smith

There was no ice cream van in Eilat.
But there was the sea.
On Saturday mornings we would go to the sea. My father
would take us.
My father never swam. He had a trauma, he said.
When he was a young boy, five years old, his older brothers
dislocated
His shoulder,
While he was swimming.
He never swam since.
But when we would go to the sea on Saturday mornings,
Father
Would bring along with him tin
Cans
Of
Snails and oysters which the sailors had brought for him.
He worked at the port as a cargo engineer. Once, when we
were with him at the sea, me
And my little brother,
We asked him to swim. He stumbled into the water until
it reached his knees.
"Look at me," he said and smiled.
He didn't smile much.
There was no ice cream van in Eilat.

And there was no rag-and-bone man.
But there were plenty of tourists sun bathing topless on
the beach
Or at the hotels' swimming pools.
On school holidays my baby brother and I would go with
Mum
To the hotel where she worked.
Once it was the Red Rock hotel and after that
Club Inn and it was always some
Hotel.
At the Red Rock Hotel I stared at these two topless bright-
Haired tourists.
I was staring at them for two whole days. I was maybe seven
years old. On the third
Day one of them stepped over me
I was lying on a blue water mattress and she stepped over
me. I smiled. She had stopped and
Stepped over me again placing
Her bare foot on my little back.
The next couple of days I would spend between her big
boobs, and her friend's boobs.
I would come early in the morning and I would wait for
them. I don't know how old they were
But I
Remember
Myself sitting on their lap and playing with their boobies
Until my older sister noticed it one day and ran and told
Mum.
There was no ice cream van in Eilat.
But at school we played that we were ancient Romans. I
would be Julius Caesar
And Dror would be
Drordorakis and Sagi would still be Siegel from that other

game when we were
Gangsters.
I would spend the afternoons mainly at home. Or at the
public library. And sometimes,
I would go
And play with my little brother. Through all those years in
Eilat, my brother and I would
Dream of other countries.
And we had that game with the swing.
We would swing high on the swing seats and we would
imagine that they were aeroplanes. I
Would be the pilot explaining
Where we were
Flying to. We would fly to Athens to see the Parthenon, to
Rome to see
The Colosseum, Eiffel Tower
In Paris and Buckingham Palace in London. We would fly
over to the Americas as well but
We didn't have anything specific to do over there
And when it would get dark Mum would call us to dinner,
shouting out of the window
And we would say
"Just a minute Mum,
We need to fly back to Eilat."
We would always dream of
Other countries.
There was no ice cream van in Eilat.
And in the winter nothing was growing.
It was just
That there was nothing green about Eilat.
When I was ten years old we moved to Herzliya.
We arrived there on the break between the fifth and sixth
grade. It was summer

And it didn't seem that different from Eilat.
In the winter everything seemed greener, especially the road leading
To Weizmann elementary school.
There were chrysanthemums and lots of grass.
In Herzliya there was a rag-and-bone man. An old cart and an old grey horse. But
It wouldn't make that big a difference
Anyway.
I clearly remember this moment, when I came down that
Leafy hill with the other kids from class,
That hill spreading from the other side of the road
In front of our school gates.
Dark cumulus drifted in the grey skies above us like the old cart of
The rag-and-bone man
And then that tune, and the white van covered with "Strauss ice cream" stickers
And photos of the many different ice creams
And popsicles.
Between the green hill and our school gates it stood
The ice cream van.

Repeater Books

is dedicated to the creation of a new reality. The landscape of twenty-first-century arts and letters is faded and inert, riven by fashionable cynicism, egotistical self-reference and a nostalgia for the recent past. Repeater intends to add its voice to those movements that wish to enter history and assert control over its currents, gathering together scattered and isolated voices with those who have already called for an escape from Capitalist Realism. Our desire is to publish in every sphere and genre, combining vigorous dissent and a pragmatic willingness to succeed where messianic abstraction and quiescent co-option have stalled: abstention is not an option: we are alive and we don't agree.